Physical Science Education

PHYSICAL SCIENCE EDUCATION

Nature and Scope

C. Naseema

SHIPRA

ISBN: 978-81-7541-636-9

First Published in India in 2012

Physical Science Education

SHIPRA PUBLICATIONS
H.O.: LG 18-19, Pankaj Central Market, Patparganj,
I.P. Ext., Delhi-110092, Tel: 91-11-2223 5152, 2223 6152
Br.Off.: 4617/18, Ansari Road, Darya Ganj,
New Delhi-110002, Tel: 6594 6453, 9810522367
E-mail: info@shiprapublications.com
www.shiprapublications.com

Contents

1
Science Teaching

1.1. What is Science?

We value Science chiefly for the practical advantages it brings with it. Generally science is taken as a body of accumulated scientific information, that is science is the investigation and interpretation of the natural phenomena which occur in our daily life. Science has accumulated facts and conceptual structure. It is the result of intellectual processes that makes discovery possible and is tool in the hands of the scientists by which the researchers and scientists investigate the *unknown*.

1.2. Nature of Science

All disciplines are open to change. Any discipline is generally accepted as a branch of knowledge which represents a body of knowledge organized around certain concepts. These basic concepts form the structure of the discipline. The idea of science as a body of knowledge is true. But science is dynamic in nature, which is researched continuously by the students and the needed changes are made in the light of new ideas. Scientific information is constantly being arranged, re-arranged and reoriented.

Each discipline has its particular approach, methods of searching and systematising information. These constitute the *methods of inquiry*. Science involves the methods of enquiry known as scientific method

The application of science to society is important as the content and process of science. The science related social problems have added third dimension to the nature of science. Thus, science has *direct and indirect relationship with man and his environment* which includes social, moral and ethical consequences.

The nature of science can be represented diagrammatically as in Fig. 1.1

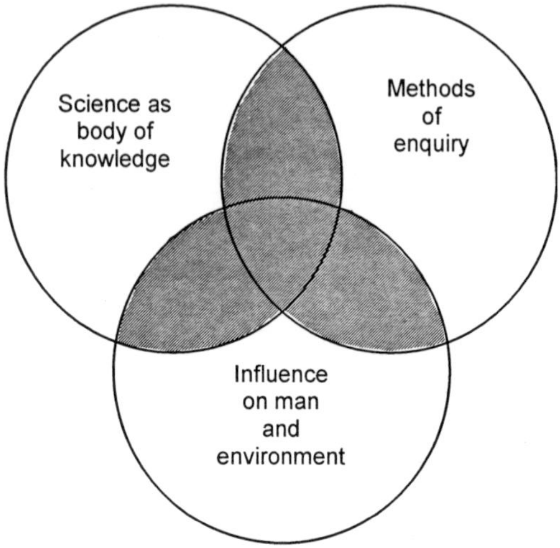

Fig. 1.1. Nature of Science

1.3. Goal of Science

One purpose of science is to produce principles and theories. A principle is a rule or law about natural phenomena – for example: "Metals expand when heated". "Cells arise only from the division of other cells". "Light is refracted toward the normal when it passes from less dense to more dense media".

A theory is more inclusive than a principle. A theory is defined as a more or less verified explanation accounting for facts or phenomena and specifying relationships between groups of empirical data. A theory has explanatory, predictive, and organizational value. For example, if you have obtained several skeletons from various strata in the earth, you will have to memorize from which level each skeleton came; but if you know the theory of evolution, you can order these skeletons (assuming they are related) and know which skeleton was obtained from the lowest stratum and the sequence of the rest of the skeletons. Knowledge of the theory of evolution aids you in understanding the relationship of the skeletons and explains their association. Knowledge of evolution helps us organize our information and makes it possible for us to make predictions. Knowing the theory of evolution enables the scientist to predict the kind of skeleton that might be found at a lower stratal depth. Atomic theory, cell theory, germ theory, and theory of evolution are but a few of the theories devised by man. A moment's reflection on their value certainly indicates why science endeavours to create these orderly explanations.

Theories are based on facts which are derived from observation and experimentation. As our experimentation progresses and reveals new information, theories often have to be modified. Scientists search for theories and principles which are true and unchanging, but the history of science has shown that there is no certainty in science but only probability. Because theories evolve and are modified as our knowledge of nature increases, the goals of science in formulating broad, encompassing ideas of knowledge – theories – never ends. There is always an assignment for the next generation.

With this realization, a scientist is humble about what he knows and thinks he knows. At first thought, it seems that the futile search for certainly would be frustrating; but there is joy in the discovery that knowledge is unending. There is always more to do and learn and more problems to solve. Life itself is a process of solving problems, and a scientist enriches his life by being involved in problems of value to all men.

1.4. Implications of Scientific Philosophy for Teaching Science

Prospective teachers seldom have research experience in science. Their college courses traditionally have offered little opportunity for them to devise an experiment or solve problems other than those of a cook-book type. Their science instruction usually has emphasized the products rather than the process of scientific research. As a result, they have generally prepared for their science classes by memorizing material. Memorization tends to emphasize the learning to be scientific. Because prospective teachers have been trained in this manner, they often mistake learning scientific words for an understanding of science. After being employed as teachers, they have emphasized memorization of terms, assuming that if a student knows scientific terms he will have more understanding of science. Teachers have falsely assumed that learning the products of science will enable a student to use the processes of science. Many scientists and science educators have become concerned with this outlook and have made efforts to produce courses and curricula which will give greater attention to the understanding of science as a process. Teachers, as a consequence, have had to become more aware of the inquiring nature of science and have had to communicate this awareness to their students.

Teaching the inquiring aspects of science requires greater understanding of scientific philosophy and considerable skill to implement it in the classroom. It is easy to pour out the facts of science – the product – but it is difficult to teach students to solve problem scientifically. A teacher who understands the philosophical bases of science and incorporates this understanding in his instruction is more likely to lead his students to modify their behaviour to face problems in scientific manner, not only in the laboratory but in life situations as well.

1.5. Need for Scientific Literacy

It is the responsibility of the schools to produce an intelligent citizenry. The ability of our citizens to understand national and international problems is dependent upon their scientific literacy. The layman is surrounded by scientific developments and is bombarded with a wealth of scientific information. Koelsche and Morgan in a study of scientific literacy report:

> "Six-month subscription were taken to 22 newspapers having the largest circulation in their geographical region of the United States and to nine of the most widely-read magazines published in this country. The subscription period was from November 1, 1962, to May 1, 1963. There were 2,999 science-oriented news items clipped from the 31 publications during this interim."

They further report that a layman reading these papers would have to know and understand 175 principles and 693 scientific words.

A literate individual must have some understanding and

appreciation of science in order to make valid judgments as citizen. Remember, national and state legislators often make decisions involving expenditures of funds for science and scientific facilities. If they were not scientifically literate, they could not make intelligent decisions. They could even be easily duped by a body of unscrupulous individuals. The significance of a lay person's making an influential decision involving science was evidenced by the experience of President Roosevelt in the World War II. A group of scientists came to him with the suggestion that the United States divert some of its badly needed resources to a project to produce an atomic bomb. This project eventually involved over US$ 2 billion in expenditures. The sum of money itself was not as significant as what it stood for in those days when raw materials were badly needed for the production of arms. What decision would President Roosevelt have made if he had had no training in science and did not understand what was being asked of him? How would the destiny of America have been changed?

All questions having to do with the expenditure of funds are relative. It is paramount that our citizens and their representatives understand the purpose and value of science, that they vote proper support for its growth, and that they make decisions based upon sound and literate understanding of science. It is our schools' responsibility to prepare the citizen for this task.

1.6. Definitions of Science

Like life, it is comparatively easier to experience Science than to define it. There are perhaps as many definitions of Science as there are scientists.

According to *Fitzpatrick,* Science is a cumulative and endless series of empirical observations which result in the formation of concepts and theories, with both concepts and theories being subject to modification in the light of further empirical observations. Science is both a body of knowledge and the process of acquiring and refining knowledge.

Dr. F.R. Schlessinger defines, "Science is a process of the human intellect. It is a way of thinking, a way of doing, a method of discovering new relationships in the physical and biological universe. It is also the product of the process'.

According to *Gilbert Archey*, Science is knowledge acquired in a particular way. It becomes a human activity, an attitude and an exercise of the mind that put us as it were in a state of familiarity with nature.

Conant defined science as, 'An interconnected series of concepts and conceptual schemes that have developed as a result of experimentation and observation and are fruitful of further experimentation and observation". These definitions emphasize three basic principles of the nature of science.

Association for Science Education defined science as, " 'science should be recognized and taught as a major human activity which explores the realms of human experience, maps it methodologically but also imaginatively, and, by disciplined speculation, creates a coherent system of knowledge'.

According to James B. Conant,

> 'science is an interconnected series of concepts and conceptual schemes that have developed as a result of experimentation and observation and are fruitful of further experimentation and observations.'

The characteristics of science are the following:

1. Science is empirical.
2. Science grows through processes of science.
3. Scientific knowledge is replicable.
4. Scientific knowledge is tentative in nature.
5. Scientific knowledge is unique as it differs from other areas of knowledge.
6. Science has its own values of objectivity, rationality and humaneness.

Science is
- a body of knowledge.
- a method of enquiry, a way of investigation.
- an attitude towards life.

Science as a Product

Whether information or ideas we acquire through various processes of Science form the body knowledge or *product* of science. Solution to every problem leads to the discovery of a new problem and the cycle goes on and on. The result is the accumulation of huge quantum of knowledge. The basic components of the *product of science are facts, concepts, principles, theories and laws*. However science is dynamic in nature. Scientific information is constantly being rearranged and reoriented in the light of new knowledge. So a person should be conscious of the ever changing nature of science.

LAW
↑
THEORIES
↑
PRINCIPLES
↑
CONCEPTS
↑
FACTS
(Product of Science)

1.7. Science as a Process

Science is more a verb than a noun. In science, *the ways of gathering information, thinking, measuring, problem solving are called processes of science*. Basic processes of science are observation, comparison, classification, communication, measurement, estimation and prediction. The abilities of prediction, explanation and generalization together form the process of making inferences. The quality of knowledge acquired in Science depends on the quality of process skills applied. Sharp observation will lead to sound and accurate knowledge. Whatever may be the problem the scientists adopt a cautious and methodological procedure that helps them to acquire valid and verifiable conclusions.

The various processes of Science can be classified into five categories.

1. Collection of data;

2. Analysis of data;
3. Synthesis of data;
4. Evaluation of data; and
5. Application of generalizations to new situations.

For learning science and understanding its process, systematic and organized use of process skills is required. Apart from the basic process skills, integrated skills are also required. Several skills function together to carry out an experiment or to solve a problem. These integrated process skills are the following:

- Identifying and controlling variables;
- Defining operationally;
- Forming hypotheses;
- Experimenting;
- Tabulating and graphing;
- Interpreting data;
- Testing hypotheses; and
- Drawing conclusions.

It is through these process skills that pupils learn to unfold the mysteries of nature. According to Dr. D.S. Kothari, "to learn Science is to do Science, there is no other way of learning Science". Science is a systematic process of learning. If Science is flourish, the whole community must understand to some degree its aims, its methods and its consequences.

1.8. Science – Both a Process and a Product

Everybody agrees that Science is both a body of knowledge and the process of acquiring it. Science is both a verb and a noun. Observing, classifying, collecting data, inferring, predicting, etc. are processes employed in the pursuit of Science. As a result of these processes we get data, facts, concepts, generalizations, principles, etc. The concept of science as both a process and a product does not over look the older view point that Science means content, but it holds that content is only a part of Science. The older view of science was concerned with what scientists knew. Now this has supplemented with what scientists do. These two aspects are interdependent and inseparable. These two aspects of

Science are often described as 'subject and method', 'content and activity', 'knowledge and behaviour', 'product and process', etc.

1.9. Aims of Teaching Physical Science

Thurber and Collette have rightly stated that, "Science can justify its place in the curriculum only when it produces important changes in young people-changes in their ways of thinking, in their habits of action and in the values they assign to what they have and what they do". The inclusion of any subject in the school curriculum depends on its utility in achieving the goals of education. The aims of teaching Physical Science in schools are:

1. Better understanding of the Nature of Science (The acquisition of knowledge)

The first and obvious reason for teaching Science is to give information about the world in which we live. The student should understand the cumulative nature of scientific knowledge. The concepts and principles are essential for an adequate understanding of the physical environment. After studying science the pupil should understand the inter-relationship and interdependence of different branches of Science.

2. Development of Scientific Attitude

Formation of scientific attitude (temper) is an important outcome of science teaching. Attitude is a condition of readiness for a certain type of activity some characteristics of scientific attitude are:

- Open-mindedness
- Curiosity
- Freedom from superstitions
- Judgment based on scientific facts alone
- Faith in cause and effect relation
- Willingness to test and verify conclusions
- Critical thinking while engaging in all activities
- Honest reporting

3. Development of Interest and Appreciation

The teaching of Science should enable the pupil develop and enjoy personal interest related to Science. Science provides opportunity for the satisfaction of pupils' desire and ultimately for the development of interest. The pupil should be able to recognize and enjoy scientific aspects of natural and man-made environment. Varied activities are included in curriculum for the development of scientific interest and appreciation.

4. Acquisition of Skills

The second valuable outcome of science education is acquisition of skills at various levels of proficiency. *Exposure to scientific knowledge both in the classroom and in the laboratory leads to the acquisition of the following skills*:

(i) *Laboratory skills or experimental skills* – e.g.: Skills for handling apparatus, observing objects and phenomena, recording the results of observations, planning experiments, preserving chemicals, improvising apparatus, etc.
(ii) *Mathematical skills* – e.g.: computation, graphing, tabulating, grading, dealing with symbols and reading tables.
(iii) *Social skills* – e.g.: to get on with people, working efficiently in groups etc.
(iv) *Safety skills* – e.g.: avoiding accidents, dong first aid when required.
(v) Drawing skills
(vi) Problem solving skills
(vii) Library skills such as locating appropriate references and consulting them.

5. Training in Scientific Method

As a result of science teaching the pupil should habitually and skillfully employ good thinking habits while confronting problems of daily life. He should be able to solve the problem by applying the scientific method. Scientific Method adopts the following steps:

- Sensing a problem
- Defining a problem
- Collecting data

- Interpreting data
- Formulating hypothesis
- Testing hypothesis
- Drawing conclusions

6. Helping the pupils adjust themselves better with the Society

Science education gives extensive practice in working together, thus promoting co-operation, tolerance, self-confidence and self-reliance among students which in turns help them to adjust with others in spite of differences of opinion.

7. Helping the pupils develop suitable Career Interests

Science can not be applied for the welfare of the society without the involvement of men and women who have been specially trained for science based vocations in industry, research and teaching. A vocational justification is therefore possible for science teaching. Science teaching should prepare the students for some vocation and specialization in the subjects and professional courses like engineering aeronautics, etc.

1.10. Instructional Objectives of Teaching Science

What is an Objective?

We have already seen that the whole educational system is directed towards realization of values and aims which lead to an all round development of pupils. An objective too is a goal towards which the learner is made to move. But as indicated above, it is immediate, specific, operationally defined and easily achievable in a limited time. Hence an objective may be said to be a part of an aim- a part that would help in gradually reaching the ultimate distant goal, that is, the aim anticipated.

An educational objective is a statement of expected results. It is a statement of what the students should be able to do at the end of learning, as compared to what they could not do beforehand.

An objective states the way in which the students will be different from what they had been, as a result of teaching. An objective defines what we are trying to accomplish by teaching. It is the terminal behaviour expected of the pupils at the conclusion of a period of learning. By clearly writing objectives what was once secret is made open for improvement and inspection.:

1.11. Principles of Curriculum Construction

While constructing curriculum in physical science, the following principles should be taken into account:

1. *Renewal Principle*: While conserving and transmitting the cultural heritage, education should cater to renewal of the culture to suit the requirements of changing times. Hence curriculum should be so constructed as to facilitate renewal of the society by infusing dynamism all aspects.
2. *Creative Principle*: God has created the universe and men have created other things in it. By nature, man is creative. Therefore, education should be so moulded as to enable one develop one's creativity. The curriculum should consist such items that would enable children to exercise their creative powers so that creativity is fostered, which in turn will enable them to modify their environment according to the needs of time.
3. *Motivation Principle*: The curriculum should be tailored to suit the needs and interests of the pupils. It must be goal directed. It should thus motivate the pupils to actively participate in the learning process with an innate desire arising out of intrinsic motivation.
4. *Maturity Principle*: The curriculum should be suited to the mental and physical maturity of the pupil.
5. *The Principle of Preparation for Life*: The school curriculum should include such elements that would prepare children for their future life. That is, they should be able to earn their livelihood sufficiently and adjust themselves with the society efficiently. It should equip the child with the calibre to meet the challenge of life.
6. *The Principle of Elasticity and Flexibility*: Since the needs of the individual and the society go on changing, a rigid and static curriculum cannot meet the requirements of the child or of the society. Moreover, experiences to be presented have to be modified to suit the environment, societal conditions, learning atmosphere, etc. Also, pupils differ

in intelligence, tastes and skills too. The curriculum by its elasticity can cater to all such requirements posed by environmental and individual differences.

7. *The Principle of Comprehensiveness*: The curriculum must be comprehensive enough to confirm to the needs of various individuals or communities. It must be broad-based to include a wide variety of subjects suited to the needs of various types of pupils and the society with all its diversities. Comprehensiveness has to be reflected also in it's potential to cater to the comprehensive or total development of an individual.
8. *The Principle of Balance*: Curriculum should maintain proper balance between direct and indirect experience, liberal and professional education, individual and social aims, compulsory and optional subjects, etc.
9. *The Principle of Utility*: Curriculum should be of practical use to the pupil, and hence should maintain vocational and technical bias. Due emphasis should be given to work experience.

In short, a curriculum should be well-balanced, properly-graded, fairly broad-based and appropriately designed for meeting the needs of the child on the one hand and those of the society, on the other.

1.12. Method of Teaching Science as Inquiry

Teaching science as inquiry places the emphases upon the student doing the learning. It encourages what John Dewey many years ago stressed- *learning by doing* and becoming actively involved in experiencing. The student is made an inquirer and is no longer allowed to be a passive observer. The emphasis has switched from the traditional teacher-centered class organization to student-centered organization. The inquiry approach requires the learner to be an active participant in the quest for knowledge. In so doing the student discovers his ability to learn *how to learn* by using his own mind to solve problems. The ability to solve problems has great value in the post-school years. Perhaps the most important thing a teacher can do is teach a student *how to learn* and instill confidence so the student can learn on his own. Oppenheimer has said, "*Research is action ... and the question is ... how to communicate this sense of action to our fellowmen who are not destined to devote their lives to the professional pursuit of new knowledge*". There is no way for a student to know the action a scientist experiences except by becoming actively involved in the methods of science. The teacher's role is one of the organizing and contriving situations which will set the stage requiring a student to act out the role of scientist in his activities. It is for this reason that the new curriculum developments devote a considerable amount of time to laboratory and field experiences. In the new courses it is not uncommon for the teacher to use four periods a week for laboratory work. Lecture, because it usually is solely informational in character, has practically no place in the instruction in these courses; however, some time is spent in discussion. The teacher asks questions, the answers to which help integrate the laboratory and text material and give general structure to the course work. In teaching by inquiry, the teacher does not act as a reservoir of stored knowledge. He seldom gives answers to questions but asks a series of questions which help the students to discover for themselves. The emphasis in instruction is on questioning, not answering – more will be said of this later in our book.

The second way a teacher gets students involved in inquiry is by giving them examples of actual scientific inquiring situations. These may be patterned after some scientist's work in solving a problem. The teacher presents background information about the problem and then involves the class in a discussion of how the problem could be solved. In the process, students follow the path a scientist used in solving it. Another way teachers instill a sense of inquiry is by becoming inquirers themselves. A teacher may not know the answer to a problem, but he may with his students study and resolve it. Students don't expect a teacher to know everything. They enjoy having their teacher involved in discovering with them some new fact or principle of science.

2
Product and Process of Science

2.1. Product of Science

The huge array of subject matter of science lying scattered consisting of innumerable facts, figures, formulae, principles, theories etc. form the product of science. The content of science is so heavy that it is impossible for one to learn it fully during his life period.

Nature of the Content of Science

Any discipline is generally accepted as a branch of knowledge which represents a body of knowledge organized around certain concepts. These basic concepts form the structure of the discipline. Each discipline has its particular approaches, methods of inquiry of the discipline. Also, a discipline is not static. It changes with the addition of new information when more specific changes come in the basic concepts which are added to the structure of the discipline.

Science is a dynamic disciplines with its own distinctiveness. Scientific information is constantly being arranged and reoriented. This is possible because, new knowledge helps in filling the gaps and old knowledge is changed in the light of new evidences. Therefore, it is said that scientific knowledge is tentative.

Science is also viewed as a method and a way of investigating. These processes are used by the scientists to search new knowledge. The new findings are based on empirical data which lay emphasis on the objectivity of its approach, analysis and inferences.

The various definitions gives to science, themselves indicate the nature of its content, that science is functional in character. Everything contained in the huge stock of scientific knowledge i.e., product of science is of course useful but not necessary for human living. Also, science contains objective and verifiable facts.

2.2. Process of Science

Process of science has been defined as the characteristics of the activities and scientist's methods of analysis. In other words, these are the methods which scientists practise while innovating or searching new knowledge, or doing laboratory work or conducting some experiment.

These processes are essential part of the learning experiences of students so that they can learn and practise the methodologies of science. The various processes of science include—the way the scientists identifies a problem, the way they learn through observation, the way they experiment, the way they formulate questions and hypotheses, the way they interpret data and draw inferences, the way apply generalizations to new situation etc. This systematic procedure of solving problem is what we call the scientific method.

2.3. Scientific Method

It is a systematic and orderly method of solving problems. Whatever be the nature of the problem, the scientists adopt a continuous and methodical procedure which helps them to acquire valid and verifiable conclusions. To give training in scientific method of solving problems, which is one of the aims of learning physical science, the teacher should provide necessary situations. Steps involved in scientific method are as follows:

1. Identifying the problem
2. Defining the problem
3. Collecting the data
4. Interpreting the data
5. Formulation of hypotheses
6. Drawing conclusion and making generalization
7. Application of generalization.

1. Identifying the Problem

The teacher can put such questions which may require reflective thinking and reasoning on the part of the students to solve. The setting up of a problem may be a co-operative approach of the teacher and students. The selected problem should be according to the need and requirements of the students.

2. Defining the Problem

The problems should be defined in concise, definite and clear language. The most essential feature of defining the problem is that, the students should be able understand the problem and grasp it.

3. Collecting Data

When the students have grasped and defined the problem they look for the possible solution. Here the teacher should help the students to collect the relevant data. The methods like field trips, discussion with experts, preparation of models or charts, observation and experiment can be used at this stage.

4. Interpreting Data

This is a difficult step. Students require a lot of practice in interpreting data. Students organize the collected data on the basis of similarity and differences and plan experiments to answer questions and test idea. The superfluous data is discarded, and the relevant data is interpreted based on the problem

5. Formulation of Hypotheses

After organizing the data, the students may be asked to write down the inferences based on the obtained evidence and to propose ways of testing out these inferences.

A hypothesis is a tentative suggestion for the solution of a problem or an explanation for some phenomenon. It is only a statement that may or may not be true.

Characteristics of a good hypothesis:

(a) A hypothesis must have explanatory power
(b) A hypothesis must be testable

(c) A hypothesis should be consistent with the existing body of knowledge.
(d) A hypothesis should be stated simply, clearly and precisely in unambiguous terms.

6. Selecting and Testing the most likely Hypothesis

The students can select the most tenable hypothesis by rejecting the others through discussions and experimentation. The selected hypothesis is again tested experimentally to find out its truth.

7. Drawing Conclusion and Making Generalization

The tested hypothesis gives an idea of the conclusion to be reached. The generalization can be made by arranging a set of experiments which also show the same conclusion already reached at.

8. Application of Generalization

The students should be able to apply the generalizations to their daily life. This would help bridge the gap between the classroom situation and real life situation.

Thus the scientific method involves a procedure of attacking the problem, finding out the solution inductively and testing the adequacy of the generalization by deductive approach.

2.4. Elements of Scientific Method

1. Induction

Inductive reasoning is moving from specific observations to broader generalizations and theories. It is 'Bottom up approach' beginning with specific observations and measures, formulate tentative hypothesis that one can explore and finally it culminates when one is able to develop some general conclusions and theories.

Induction requires careful examination of particular facts and examples to enable one deduce a general principle or rule. Induction is accepting a universal truth if it is found true of any particular case and again true of a reasonable number of similar cases. Then it is presumed that it will be true for all cases. A formula or generalization is thus arrived at through a convincing processing of reasoning made on the basis of a number of particular cases

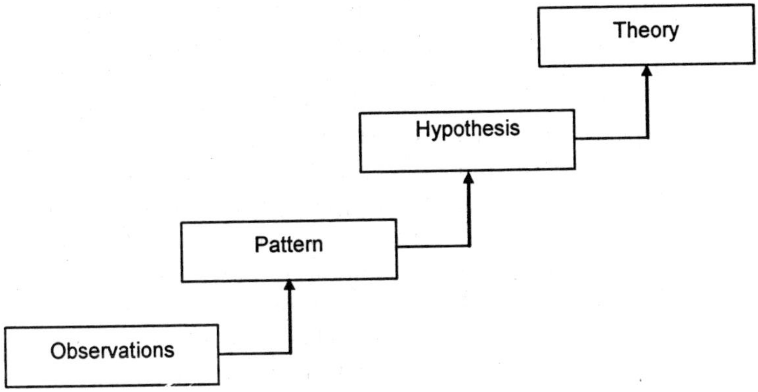

that exhibit similarity or commonality. Inductive inferences are based on two assumptions:

(i) *The law of uniformity of nature*: A phenomenon that takes place in certain circumstances will repeat itself whenever the same circumstances occur.

(ii) *The law of causation*: Every phenomenon has a cause or a set of causes that is invariably connected with it. In other words nothing takes place in the world by sheer chance.

Often it is difficult to decide all the possible causes and to find conclusive reasons. In complex cases where there is a plurality of causes, it is difficult to decide what is the cause and what is the effect. In such cases we try to establish the causal relation by adopting one of the following five methods known as Mill's five canons of induction.

The following are the canons:

1. *The method of agreement*: If, in every observed instance of a phenomenon only one factor or circumstance is common, then that factor or circumstance is probably the case of that phenomenon.
   The conclusion obtained by this method is not decisive. Unless a number of varied instances are considered, and all other causal circumstance eliminated, the method leads to absurd inferences.
2. *The method of difference*: Whenever the elimination of a

single circumstance is accompanied by the non-occurrence of a phenomenon that circumstance is probably related to its causation.

The method of difference is very largely used in experimental science. Each of our activities produces an effect and when the effect is absent in the absence of the activity, the activity is considered the cause of the effect. In this method we compare two instances, one in which the phenomenon occurs and other in which it does not.

3. *The joint method*: This is a combination of the methods of agreement and differences. The suggestion of causation arrived at by the method of agreement is strengthened by the method of difference. The application of this joint method leads of fairly valid conclusions.
4. *The method of residues*: If part of a complex phenomenon is known to be causally related to certain operating circumstances, the residual part of the phenomenon must be due to the rest of the relevant circumstances (known or unknown). This method does not necessarily determine what the cause is. But it helps to limit the field of enquiry so as to make it easier to hit on a hypothesis that could be tested out.
5. *The method of concomitant variations*: If two phenomena vary concomitantly, while all other relevant circumstances remain unchanged, they must be causally related.

These methods of induction suggested by Mill are applicable only to cases that can be perceived by the senses. They cannot be applied to more hidden laws which really express the most fundamental relations of nature.

2. Deduction

Deduction or deductive reasoning is when one proceeds from general to specific aspects using prescribed rules of logic. A formula or definition is accepted by the individual as a well established truth for interpreting a specific problematic situation. Deductive reasoning works from the more general to the more specific. It is 'Top-down approach' beginning with thinking up a theory about the topic of interest. Then narrowing down that into more specific hypothesis that one can test, and then narrowing it down even further when one can collect observations to address the hypothesis. This ultimately leads one to be able to test the hypothesis with specific data – confirmation (or not) of the original theory (or theories).

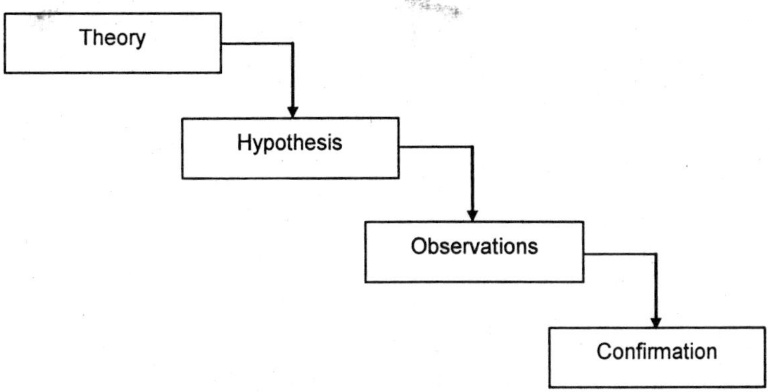

Deduction operates through a series of statements known as syllogisms containing three parts viz., (i) the major premise or statement on which reasoning is based (ii) the minor premise, and (iii) the conclusion.

Illustration (1)

(a) Mammals suckle their young ones (Major premise)
(b) Bat is a mammal (Minor premise); therefore
(c) Bat suckles its young ones (Conclusion)

In deduction if the premises are true, the conclusion is necessarily true. Deductive reasoning is useful as it provides a means for linking theory and observation.

Deductive methods give speed, skill and efficiency in the solution of the problem. In deduction one has to memorize large number of formulae and rules. It is very difficult for the beginner to understand an abstract piece of work if not preceeded by a number of concrete instances.

3. *Analogy*

Scientific methods make use of analogy also in drawing inferences in scientific investigations. Whenever we perceive a new object or event the first impulse of the mind is to compare and connect it with the nearly similar previous experiences. When two objects or phenomena are similar in some respects, we anticipate that they would be similar in other respects also. The recognition of analogy is helpful in apprehending new experiences and suggesting causal relations. The conclusions arrived at by analogical reasoning are much less probable than those of induction or deduction.

4. Analysis and Synthesis

All the methods of inference are made possible only by the mental process of analysis and synthesis. They form the real foundation of the scientific method. Analysis means separating into meaningful parts and synthesis means putting them together. In induction observed facts are analysed and they are synthesized into relationships. In deduction we analyse a general proposition and synthesise the relevant facts to explain particular cases. Analysis and synthesis are extremely important in the study of a phenomenon having plurality of cases or characteristics.

5. Hypothesis

Hypothesis making and testing are the two integrated processes which play an important role in scientific enquiry. Hypotheses are tentative solutions or shrewed guesses that are formulated and provisionally adopted to explain observed facts or to propose probable solutions, which in turn act as a guide to further investigation. Hypothesis is the most important mental technique of the investigator. Its main function is to suggest new ways of argument, experiments or new observations. A hypothesis serves as a powerful beacon that throws light along the way for the investigator to proceed. Analogy and simple methods of induction are helpful in forming hypothesis. The breadth of knowledge, experience as well as imaginative insight of the investigator are helpful in the formation of hypothesis. So the investigator should have wide reading, familiarity with existing practices and first hand contact with the pertinent data. Hypothesis provides direction to research. It tells the investigator what to do and how to proceed.

Characteristics of a Good Hypothesis

1. A good hypothesis must be based directly on existing data.
2. It must have explanatory power-explain existing data in simpler forms.
3. It must be consistent with universal laws which have been established beyond doubt.
4. It should be testable i.e., deductions, conclusions or inferences can be drawn on the basis of the hypothesis.
5. It should be simple, stated clearly and precisely in unambiguous terms.

2.5. Transfer of Training and the Scientific Method

When the training in one situation or one form of activity affects one's ability in other fields of activity, it is said to be transfer of training. Skills obtained in one field or performance in one task can influence one's performance in other fields or task. It is hoped that the training obtained through the scientific method can be utilized in solving the problems of our life. Hence it is desirable that scientific technique in thinking is developed in students for dealing with problematic situations efficiently and successfully. Students should be made to understand the advantages of the scientific method and impressive achievements of great scientists so that they might be inspired to adopt the same type of methodical procedure to solve problems related to their day today activities.

2.6. Science as an Attitude

Science can also be regarded as an attitude. The acquisition of scientific attitude is one of the most important outcomes of learning Science. A person with scientific attitude will have the following attributes.

- Open mindedness
- Curiosity
- Belief in cause and effect relationship
- Freedom from superstitious
- Intellectual honesty
- Objectivity
- Willingness to change beliefs

- Respect of others' opinion if convincing
- Judgment based on scientific facts
- Critical mindedness

A science teacher can, by setting his example, helps to develop these characteristics in his students.

3
Aims and Objectives of Teaching Physical Science

Science and technology affects all aspects of life and thus, we should have decision making ability to judiciously choose and use science and technology that is useful for our society. As a nation, India is heading for rapid industrialization based on the use of high-technology. Such efforts require highly trained experts and scientifically literate citizens.

3.1. Difference between Aims and Objectives

Many times these terms are used interchangeably. But aims refer to more general ultimate goals. Goals are broad and long term and present ultimate purpose. Aims are more specific than goals. Objectives are much more specific than aims. Purposes, outcomes and objectives, generally convey the same meaning.

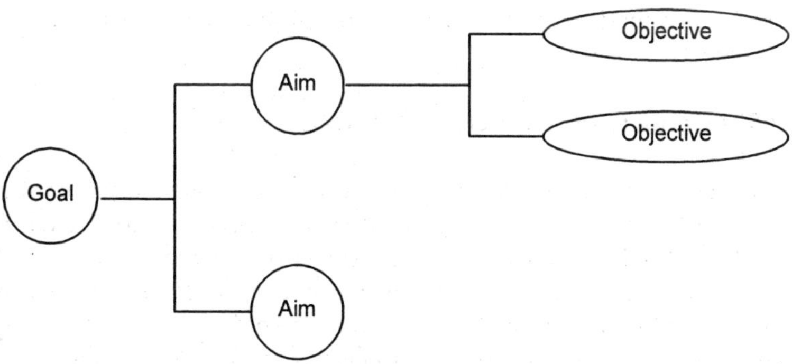

Fig. 3.1. Relationship among Goals, Aims and Objectives

Figure 3.1 showing relationship among goals, aims and objectives as presented in UNESCO Handbook (1980).

Aims of Science Teaching

According to NPE (1986) "education is essentially for the all round development of the learner both material and spiritual". Also, "Science education will be strengthened to develop in the child well-defined abilities and values such as the spirit of enquiry, creativity, objectivity the courage to question and the aesthetic sensitivity'.

3.2. Objective Based Instruction

An instructional objective is a specific and immediate goal attainable as a result of instruction. In that respect, instructional objectives differ from educational aims. Aims such as 'self realization', 'personality development', etc. are distant and too general. They are not fully realizable within a limited time span. But objectives can be realized. For example, the objective 'developing understanding on a concept' can be fully realized within a very limited time. Hence these are more crucial for a practicing teacher. When properly stated, instructional objectives serve as a guide for both teaching and evaluation. A clear description of the intended outcome of instruction helps the teacher in selecting relevant materials and methods of instruction, in monitoring pupil's learning progress, and in selecting and practicing appropriate evaluation procedures. The instruction which is aimed to attain the pre-determined objectives is known as objective based instruction.

3.3. Taxonomy of Instructional Objectives

The taxonomy of instructional objectives is basically classification scheme that is similar in form to the classification system used in Biology. The idea of taxonomy of instructional objectives emerged at an informal meeting of college examiners attending the American Psychological Association Convention (APAC) at Boston in 1948. It was agreed upon to classify instructional objectives under three domains – Cognitive, Affective, and Psychomotor.

What is a Domain?

A domain simply means category. Taxonomy is a structure, a plan, or a checklist to assist in planning and training to cover each development stage of the learner's growth. It is important that each stage is mastered before moving on to the next stage.

Cognitive domain includes those objectives which deal with the development of intellectual abilities related to the acquisition, processing and mastery of knowledge.

Affective domain includes those objectives which are concerned with desirable modifications in the emotional patterns related to appreciation, interests, attitudes, values, etc.

Psychomotor domain includes the development of manipulative or motor skills.

Based on the above decision, a team of professors headed by Dr. Benjamin S. Bloom of the University of Chicago (USA) developed books on 'Taxonomy of Educational Objectives' in 1956. These taxonomies are often referred to as *Bloom's Taxonomy*. Bloom served as the editor for the work while the book was actually the work of a large team of researchers. The first among the taxonomies published was *The Taxonomy of the Educational Objective: Cognitive Domain*. This work was the first real effort to identify what learning really was. It established a set of educational goals related to changes in the cognitive area—remembering, recalling knowledge, thinking, and problem solving and creating. The taxonomy is organized into six major classes of hierarchical order namely—knowledge, comprehension, application, analysis, synthesis and evaluation.

I. Cognitive Domain

As already pointed out, the cognitive domain involves knowledge and development of intellectual tasks. This includes the recall or recognition of specific facts, terms, symbols, concepts, procedural patterns, etc. that serve as the basis for the development of ability for intellectual activities. There are six hierarchical levels of learning in this domain. The levels indicate the level of complexity and hence difficulty in processing the knowledge.

II. Affective Domain

In 1964, Krathwohl, Bloom and others listed the major categories of modification of the affective domain. Changes in this domain indicate the manner in which one deals with situations involving feelings, interests, attitudes, appreciations, values, etc.

III. Psychomotor Domain

The categories of modifications in the psychomotor domain have been listed by R.H. Dave's in 1970. These include:

(i) Imitation
(ii) Manipulation
(iii) Precision
(iv) Articulation
(v) Naturalization

To overcome the limitations of Dave's classification Simpson and others listed the major categories of the behaviours of the psychomotor domain in 1972. The psychomotor behaviours include physical movement, co-ordination, and the use of the motor-skills. Development of these skills requires practice and is measured in terms of speed, precision, distance, procedure, or techniques in execution.

3.4. Major Categories in the Cognitive Domain (Bloom and Others, 1956)

1. *Knowledge*: Knowledge is defined as the remembering of previously learned material. This may involve the recall of a wide range of materials, from specific facts to complete theories, but all that is required is the bringing to mind of the appropriate information. Knowledge represents the lowest level of learning outcomes in the cognitive domain.
2. *Comprehension*: Comprehension is defined as the ability to grasp the meaning of material. This may be shown by translating material from one form to another (words or numbers), by interpreting material (explaining or summarizing), and by estimating future trends (predicting consequences or effects). These learning outcomes go one step beyond the simple remembering of material, and represent the lowest level of understanding.

3. *Application*: Application refers to the ability to use learned material in new and concrete situations. This may include the application of such things as rules, methods, concepts, principles, laws, and theories. Learning outcomes in this area require a higher level of understanding than those under comprehension.
4. *Analysis*: Analysis refers to the ability to break down material into its component parts so that its organizational structure may be understood. This may include the identification of the parts, analysis of the relationships between parts, and recognition of the organizational principles involved. Learning outcomes here represent a higher intellectual level than comprehension and application because they require an understanding of both the content and the structural form of the material.
5. *Synthesis*: Synthesis refers to the ability to put parts together to form a new whole. This may involve the production of a unique communication (theme or speech), a plan of operations (research proposal), or a set of abstract relations (scheme for classifying information). Learning outcomes in this area stress creative behaviours, with major emphasis on the formulation of new patters or structures.
6. *Evaluation*: Evaluation is concerned with the ability to judge the value of material (statement, novel, poem, research report) for a given purpose. The judgements are to be based on definite criteria. These may be internal criteria (organization) or external criteria (relevance to the purpose) and the student may determine the criteria or be given them. Learning outcomes in this area are highest in the cognitive hierarchy because they contain elements of all of the other categories, plus value judgments based on clearly defined criteria.

3.5. Major Categories in the Affective Domain (Krathwohl, Bloom and Others, 1964)

1. *Receiving*: Receiving refers to the student's willingness to attend to particular phenomena or stimuli (classroom activities, textbook, music, etc.). From a teaching

Table 3.1: Levels Under Objectives of Cognitive Domain

Objectives		*Levels*
1. Knowledge	The ability to recall or recognize facts, rules or concepts	- Knowledge of specifics - Knowledge of ways and means of dealing with specifics - Knowledge of the universals and abstractions in the field
2. Comprehension	The ability to understand facts and concepts	- Translation - Interpretation - Extrapolation
3. Application	The ability to apply knowledge gained, in new situations	- Use of rules - Use of methods - Use of concepts
4. Analysis	The ability to identify components of a whole and see how they are interrelated	- Analysis of elements - Analysis of relationships - Analysis of principles
5. Synthesis	The ability to integrate components to form a new whole.	- Production of a unique communication - Planning - Derivation of a set of abstract relations
6. Evaluation	The ability to judge and compare procedures, products, etc.	- Judgements using internal evidence - Judgements using external criteria

standpoint, it is concerned with getting, holding and directing the student's attention. Learning outcomes in this area range from the simple awareness that a thing exists to selective attention on the part of the learner. Receiving represents the lowest level of learning outcomes in this area range from the simple awareness that a thing exists to selective attention on the part of the learner. Receiving represents the lowest level of learning outcomes in the affective domain.

2. *Responding*: Responding refers to active participation on the part of the student. At this level he not only attends to a particular phenomenon but also reacts to it in some way. Learning outcomes in this area may emphasize acquiescence in responding (reads assigned material), willingness to respond (voluntarily reads beyond assignment), or satisfaction in responding (reads for

pleasure or enjoyment). The higher levels of this category include those instructional objectives that are commonly classified under *interest*; that is, those that stress the seeking out and enjoyment of particular activities.

3. *Valuing*: Valuing is concerned with the worth or value a student attaches to a particular object, phenomenon, or behaviour. This ranges in degree from the more simple acceptance of a value (desires to improve group skills) to the more complex level of commitment (assumes responsibility for the effective functioning of the group). Valuing is based on the internalization of a set of specified values expressed in the student's overt behaviour. Learning outcomes in this area are concerned with behaviour that is consistent and stable enough to make the value clearly identifiable. Instructional objectives that are commonly classified under attitudes and appreciation would fall into this category.
4. *Organization*: Organization is concerned with bringing together different values, resolving conflicts between them, and beginning the building of an internally consistent value system. Thus the emphasis is on comparing, relating and synthesizing values. Learning outcomes may be concerned with conceptualization of a value (recognized the responsibility of each individual for improving human relations) or with the organization of a value system (develops a vocational plan that satisfies his need for both economic security and social service). Instructional objectives relating to the development of philosophy of life would fall into this category.
5. *Characterization by a Value or Value Complex*: At this level of the affective domain, the individual has a value system that has controlled his behaviour for a sufficiently long time for him to have developed a characteristic life style. Thus, the behaviour is pervasive, consistent, and predictable. Learning outcomes at this level cover a broad range of activities, but the major emphasis is on the fact that the behaviour is typical or characteristic of the student. Instructional objectives that are concerned with the student's general patterns of adjustment (personal, social, emotional) would be appropriate here.

Examples of Specific Instructional Objectives for the Affective Domain

Specific Instructional Objectives	*Specific Learning Outcomes*
Listens attentively Shows sensitivity to social problems Accepts differences of race and culture Attends closely to the classroom activities	Asks, chooses, describes, follows, gives, holds, identifies, locates, names, points to, selects, sits erect, replies, uses.
Completes assigned homework/ obey school rules/ Participates in class discussion/ Completes laboratory work/ Volunteers for special tasks/ Shows interest in subject/ Enjoys helping other	answer, assists, complies, conforms, discusses, greets, helps, labels, performs, practices, presents, reads, recites, reports, selects, tells, writes
Demonstrates belief in the democratic process Appreciates good literature (art or music) Appreciates the role of science (or other subjects) in everyday life Shows concern for the welfare of others Demonstrates problem-solving attitude Demonstrates commitment to social improvement	completes, describes, differentiates, explains, follows, forms, initiates, invites, joins, justifies, proposes, reads, reports, selects, shares, studies, works.
Recognizes the need for balance between freedom and responsibility in a democracy Recognize the role of systematic planning in solving problems Accepts responsibility for own behaviour Understands and accepts own strength and limitations	Adheres, alters, arranges, combines, compares, completes, defends, explains, generalizes, identifies, integrates, modifies, orders, organizes, prepares, relates, synthesizes
Displays safety consciousness Demonstrates self-reliance in working independently Practices co-operation in group activities Uses objective approach in problem solving Demonstrates industry and self-discipline Maintains good health habits	Acts, discriminates, displays, influences listens, modifies, performs, practices, proposes, qualifies, questions, revises, serves, solves, uses, verifies.

3.6. Major Categories under Psychomotor Domain

Besides Bloom, there are several other noted learning theorists that explain this domain. The four primary domains have been developed by RH Dave (1967), E J Simpson (1972), A J Harrow (1972), and A Romiszowski. Dave's Psychomotor Domain is the simplest domain and easy to apply in a corporate environment. The Psychomotor Domains defined by Harrow and Simpson are better suited for certain adult training and for teaching young adults and children.

The table below compares each of the Psychomotor Domains.

Dave	*Simpson*	*Harrow*	*Romiszowski*
None	Perception (awareness)	Reflex Movement	Acquiring Knowledge
Imitation (copy)	Set	Basic Fundamental Movements	Executing Actions
Manipulation	Guided Response	Perceptual Abilities	Transfer
Develop Precision	Mechanism	Physical Abilities	Automatization
Articulation	Complex Overt Response	Skilled Movements	Generalization
Naturalization	Adaptation	Non-discursive	None
None	Origination	none	None

Dave's Classification of Objectives under Psychomotor Domain (1975)

- *Imitation*: Observing and patterning behaviour after someone else. Performance may be of low quality. Example: Copying a work of art.
- *Manipulation*: Being able to perform certain actions by following instructions and practicing. Example: Creating work on one's own, after taking lessons, or reading about it.
- *Precision*: Refining, becoming more exact. Few errors are apparent. Example: Working and reworking something, so it will be "just right."

- *Articulation*: Coordinating a series of actions, achieving harmony and internal consistency. Example: Producing a video that involves music, drama, colour, sound, etc.
- *Naturalization*: Having high level performance become natural, without needing to think much about it. Examples: Michael Jordan playing basketball, Nancy Lopez hitting a golf ball, etc.

Example

The following is an example of a lesson applying Dave's Psychomotor Domain to teach a psychical behaviour such as the sport of jumping rope.

Learning Task: Concepts of jump rope, advantages of jumping rope, and instructions for rhythmic jumping rope skills

Learning Objectives:

- Student will demonstrate three basic jump rope skills
- Student will show rhythmic coordination by participating in jump rope activities

Steps	*Instructor*	*Student*	*Type of Instruction*
Imitation	• Impart content knowledge • Demonstrate the entire skill without interruptions • Demonstrate basic jumping rope skills • Provide student opportunity to "imitate"	• Student listens to instructor • Student observes the instructor • Student attempts to imitate instructor	• Explanation • Demonstration • Guided practice
Manipulation	• Break skill into step-by-step actions, explain each step • Start in position - Swing rope - Jump over rope	• Student tries specific steps over and over • Student tries entire skill	• Guided practice • Feedback

(*Contd.*)

Steps	*Instructor*	*Student*	*Type of Instruction*
	• Provide student opportunity to "imitate" each step • Provide student opportunity to "imitate" entire skill		
Precision	• Provide student time to practice alone	• Student practices until able to perform with no mistakes • Student practices skill over and over • Student speeds up performance	• Practice alone
Articulation	• Provide student time to practice alone	• Student creates jump rope routine to music • Student fine tunes performance	• Practice alone • Practice with music
Naturalization	• Assess student's entire performance	• Student creates his or her own routine to music • Student can perform jumping rope during upon demand • Student goes from being a novice to an expert	• Assessment

3.7. Specific Objectives

Mention has already been made about analyzing each educational objective into more specific objectives. Since this is a very important aspect in objective-based instruction a more detailed discussion on these is attempted below:

An objective is a level of mental growth which the learner attains as a result of action and reaction related to learning activities provides. This means that learning results in some change in the behaviour of the learner and these behavioural changes can be taken as the evidences of the attainment of an objective. These evidences are observable and measurable. The observable and measurable behavioural changes as a result of realizing an objective is termed as specific objectives or specifications. This can be compared with the measurement of temperature. Temperature is not directly measurable, but we collect evidences of it such as the expansion of mercury due to rise in temperature. So the expansion of a substance is observable and measurable, but we collect evidences of it such as the expansion of mercury due to rise in temperature. So the expansion of a substance is observable and measurable evidence to assess the temperature. Even the hotness can be taken as an evidence of temperature but it is not exactly measurable. Similarly the teacher can determine the level of achievement of any specific educational objective from the observable and measurable behavioural changes resulting from the realization of the major objective. It is an important thing that, an objective can have more than one specification. For example, if one has acquired knowledge of a term he will be able to (i) recall it's meaning (ii) recognize it from others. The specific objectives are also known as performance objectives, behavioural objectives, and measurable objectives or merely specifications.

Criteria for Writing Major Instructional Objectives

The following criteria should be kept in mind while writing instructional objectives.

1. *The statement of objective should contain a non-action verb.* For example:
   (i) The learner acquires knowledge of the various branches of science.
   (ii) The learner develops skill in manipulating apparatus
   Here the verbs "acquires" and "develops" are non action verbs which we cannot measure or observe directly.
2. *The statement should indicate a worthwhile objective.* By worthwhile objectives what we mean is that the objectives is directed towards desirable progressive changes and could be achieved by way of teaching science.

3. *The statement should be in the form of student's achievement and not in the form of teacher's intention.* For example, it is not advisable to write: 'To develop understanding about the functions of liver among the learners. It is better to write as "The learner develops understanding about the functions of liver".
4. *The objective should be written in the form of the achievement of every single learner and not in the form of achievement of a group of learners.* For example, it is not advisable to write as "The learners apply skill in preparing the model of liver'. Instead it is better to write as 'The learner applies skill in preparing the model of liver'.
5. *The statement of objective should contain only one ability to be developed or achieved or modified.* For example, to write 'The learner acquires knowledge and applies his understanding to prepare model of liver' is a wrong usage. A better version of it is:
   (i) The learner acquires knowledge about liver.
   (ii) The learner applies the knowledge to prepare a model of liver.

Criteria for Writing Specifications

The criteria to be followed while writing specifications are given below:

1. *The statement of specification should contain an action verb.* For example, 'The learner defines the term Genetics'. Here 'defines' is the action verb.
2. *The statement of specification should contain two parts. A modification part and content part.* For example, in the specific objective, the learner defines "Genetic Engineering"; "defines" is the modification part and "Genetic Engineering" is the content part.
3. *The other criteria which are applicable to statement of major instructional objectives are applicable here also.* They are
   (i) The statement of specification should indicate a worthwhile specification.
   (ii) The statement of specification should be in the form of learner's achievement.

(iii) Statement of specification should be written in the form of the achievement of every single learner.

(iv) Specification should contain only one behaviour to be developed or modified.

(v) Specification should reflect the general characteristics warranted, namely specificity, observability and measurability.

4
Providing Learning Experiences in Science

4.1. Nature of Learning

Learning must be differentiated from related concepts such as thinking, behaviour, development or change. Learning is an internal, cognitive event that cannot be equated with observable performance. It is true that learning increases capacity for performance, that we must observe changes in performance to infer that learning has occurred. Certain kinds of learning, especially motor learning, are refined through practice. The absence of a particular behaviour does not mean that the person does not know anything about it, and the disappearance of a behaviour observed in the part does not mean that the ability to perform it has been lost.

Learning involves change, but only some kinds of changes qualify as learning. Learning is a complex process. The following definition of learning draw attention to the complexity and the nature of the process.

"Learning is the process by which an organism, as a result of its interaction in a situation, acquires a new mode of behaviour, which tends to persist and affect the general behavioural pattern of the organism, to some degree".

4.2. Principles of Learning

There are certain broad principles which are found common in learning. They are given below.

(i) Proceed from Known to Unknown

Previous experiences are of special advantages to the science teacher because his subject matter in the environment of the child itself. Learning will be effective, impressive, and meaningful to the child if sufficient correlation is male with the previous experiences of the child.

(ii) Proceed from Easy to Difficult

If the child is over burdened with complicated principles and concepts from the very beginning he get frustrated soon develops an aversion for the subject matter.

(iii) Proceed from Psychological to Logical

The logic of subject becomes sometimes indigestible for the child. The child need mastery of simple facts before proceeding to difficult ones. For example, in physical science, the inclusion of water before oxygen and hydrogen is better. But at the higher stages logical treatment can be adopted.

(iv) Proceed from Concrete to Abstract

Children need concrete experiences for effective learning. At lower stage, they are incapable of abstract thinking. The teacher must find and provide concrete experiences for the students to make them understand the abstract ideas presented in the book. For example, 'beautiful objects' are concrete in nature whereas 'beauty' is an abstract idea.

(v) Proceed from Particular to General

Learning science is not merely for the acquisition of knowledge, but to provide mental training for scientific thinking. For this, inductive (generalizing from particular examples) and deductive (extension of general idea to particular example) reasoning became inevitable. Inductive thinking has importance at the lower stages of learning and deductive thinking at the higher stages.

4.3. Interest in Learning

Everyone possesses certain interests due to which he likes certain activities or prefers to spend his leisure hours in a certain manner. What a person is interested in would be pursued even without external pressure.

Keller (1983) presented the following few strategies for stimulating and maintaining student interest and curiosity in learning.

(i) Use novel, incongruous, conflictual or paradoxical events. Attention is aroused when there is an abrupt change in the status quo.
(ii) Use anecdotes and other devices to inject a personal, emotional element into otherwise purely intellectual or procedural material.
(iii) Give students the opportunity to learn more about things they already know about, but also give them moderate doses of the unfamiliar.
(iv) Use analogies to make the strange familiar and the familiar strange.
(v) Guide students into a process of question generation and inquiry.

4.4. Motivation and Learning

Teaching success depends on the ability to motivate students to learn. Motivation is a significant variable in the learning process.

A motive is defined as any condition that initiates and sustains individual's behaviour. Drive and goal are two functional constituents of motives. Drive means the internal process that stimulate individuals to act. Goals are established by the learner who assumes the presence of a reward.

Motivation is the term used to describe what energize a person and what directs his activity.

Intrinsic and Extrinsic Motivation

Motivation may be either extrinsic or intrinsic. If a science student finds the material so meaningful that he desires to work through sheer interest, learning has its own reward. This motivation from within is called intrinsic motivation.

Extrinsic motivation is related to the rewards, gain or approval an individual wants through some activity or action.

Science teachers should place great emphasis on intrinsic motivation, positive motives such as curiosity, competence etc. The science teacher should take care of the following:

(a) Involving students in learning activity;
(b) Creating interest in learning ;
(c) Generating proper learning environment; and
(d) Generating and stimulating the curiosity of the learner.

4.5. Individualization in Learning

International Dictionary of Education defines individualized instruction as "that tailored to the needs of individual students and situations characterized by such features as clear objectives or outcome specification; active responding or frequent monitoring .... Immediate and frequent feedback, use of self paced learning ...."

Individualization in learning is an arrangement which makes it possible to provide the appropriate education for the learners. This method adjusts the education of the individual to cater to his or her specific needs or special circumstances.

The important characteristics of individualized construction are as follows:

(a) It is self-paced learning.
(b) It has provision for immediate and frequent feedback.
(c) The material to be taught must be broken down into smaller units called modules.
(d) This method can be used a reinforcement tool, and for remedial purposes.
(e) This method is suitable for distance learning.

Opportunities for Individualization

Teachers need to interact individually with students to assess their interests and needs and help them adjust their expectations appropriately. The following instruction techniques can be used for motivating students.

(a) *Learning Centres:* Teachers can make time to meet with individuals or small groups through the effective use of independent learning assignments-work done at a special place in the room, such as a learning center. Teachers might set up one or two activity centres where students complete assigned tasks on a predetermined schedule or to which students can go when they finish assignments.

(b) *Computer Use*: Assignments to be done using computers provide another way to structure more time for teachers to interact with individuals or small groups. Besides facilitating the cognitive learning of individual students, micro computers can be used to facilitate social interactions in small group assignments on selected topics.

(c) *Peer Tutoring*: Peer tutoring can be useful strategy for helping the teacher individualize learning and motivate student behaviour. Both the students who receives help and the student who provides it can benefit.

Tutor often gain as much as the student being tutored. The extra review of material they teach and the additional practice they get while tutoring are likely to increase their own knowledge or skills.

If the tutoring focuses on cognitive skills that are important rather than on exercises that just kill time, and if the tutor and the one being tutored know and understand their roles, tutoring can be a valuable instructional and motivational aid.

4.6. Concretization in Learning

Piaget's (1983) theory on cognitive development shows that concrete objects, diagrams, charts, and other visual aids facilitate learning and learning required active response.

If what the child learning is what he do, he must actually practice the doing, acting it out in behaviour or at least formulating a plan in his own words. Just watching and listening will result in 'merely verbal' learning rather than meaningful learning.

Concretization helps students to bridge the gap between the known and the unknown, thus increasing the degree to which new material is relatively understandable. In physical science classes for example, laboratory demonstrations illustrate literally the abstract principles being taught.

Concept Formation

As mentioned earlier, a concept is a set of objects, symbols or events that share common characteristics. Concepts formation involves identifying the defining attribution of concept that can be generalized to new examples and used to discriminate valid examples of the concept from non examples.

Instructional designers typically call for sequencing material from the simple to the complex and that research on concept learning suggests first stating the concept *delimitation* and identifying its defining attributes, next presenting positive examples, and then presenting negative examples. But there are exceptions. Case and Bereiter (1984) noted the value of starting with learners current concepts and preconceptions. Other investigators suggested beginning with basic-level categories and then working both upwards and downwards from there, rather than starting with simpler concept that represent subordinate-level categories.

Clark (1971) reviewed the concept of teaching literature and concluded that instruction should begin with *positive introductory examples* next move to *positive confirmatory examples* and then move to *negative examples*.

For example: The concept of 'square'. positive introductory examples Illustrates the definition attributes and Possible irrelevant attributes

Positive introductory examples

(i) Four sides (ii) All sides of equal length	defining attributes
(iii) All corners right angles	
(iv) How a square is oriented in space (v) Size of the square	irrelevant attribute

Positive confirmatory examples contain all of the defining attributes but in addition display irrelevant attributes. Positive confirmatory examples for 'square' include squares of varying sizes and spatial rotations.

Negative examples lack one or more of the defining attributes. For 'square' a picture of an elephant is a negative example.

Plateaus in Learning

Ebbinghaus (1885) was the first to note the relationship between time and learning. He showed that increases in practice time led to increases in performing. Graphs illustrating these relationships are the *learning curves*. Ebbinghaus also illustrated forgetting curves. Forgetting is rapid in the early minutes and hours following learning but much slower thereafter.

The rate of the growth of learning can be quantitatively measured by plotting it on a curve. If we plot the period spent in learning or the number of trials for learning on the 'X' axis and increases in skill or performance on 'Y' axis, the plot will be as in Fig. 4.1.

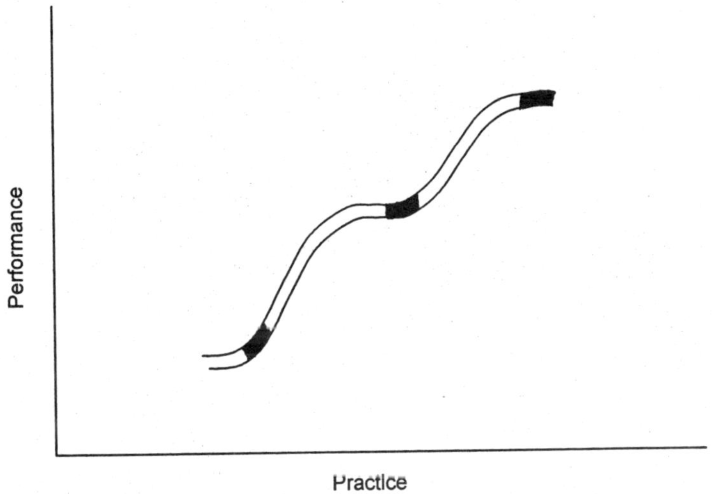

Fig. 4.1. Learning Curve – Theoretical

Fig. 4.1 represents a theoretical curve. The different stages in learning curve are shown in black and white lines.

Initial lag: Learning begins with a period of no gains in the beginning. Learning does take place during this period, but it is not visible.

Increasing gains: The period of initial lag is followed by a period of increased gains. There is a sudden growth in the rate of learning. The learner gets new insight as a result of his orientation to the task and has strong motivation to gain in learning.

Decreasing gains: The period of increasing gains is followed by a decrease in the rate of learning. The rate of learning is slowed down. This is could be due to many factors; the learner may have gained so far and has to spend some energy and time in maintaining these gains. A sense of satisfaction of achievement during the earlier period may also slow down the rate.

Plateau: This is the most critical period in learning. This is the period of little or no gain in learning. During this period the learner feels, and the observer also has a feeling that no progress is made with practice. This is a flat portion on a hill where one walks but not climb.

Several factors may cause the plateau stage; the plateau may show that the pupil is having some difficulty in learning. This may sometimes indicate that the student is taking time of initial lag to start again. Plateau may also be caused by temporary loss of motivation or loss of interest.

The teacher should find out when the period of plateau is reached. He can then take steps to reduce this period, or even to eliminate it by finding out the possible causes and remedying them. Some of the measures useful in this regard are improving the method of teaching, increasing motivation, helping the learner to get over difficulty, changing patterns of practice on the task and so forth.

End Spurt: After a period of no apparent gain, there is an increase in learning. The gain at the plateau period may be more hidden which is shown in the period following the plateau. This shows that learning continues, although at a slower rate.

4.7. Problems arising from Heterogeneous Classrooms

Individual and group differences among students have implications for classroom management. Differences in age, gender, need, interest etc. come readily to mind along with variables such as maturity and responsibility. Well established gender differences, for example, indicate that boys are more physically active than girls, at least during childhood, so that tight restrictions on movement are more difficult for them. The combination of sustained attention and physical immobility is especially difficult for younger students, regardless of gender.

Characteristics that vary across groups or cultures also may have implication for classroom management. Many adolescents resent being touched in any way. Teachers also may anger students by taking away or otherwise overreacting to articles of clothing, combs, or other valued possessions. It is important for teachers to be aware of such cultural differences and be more open minded and tolerant in dealing with students from different cultural backgrounds.

Most of the problems that teachers deal with are essentially trivial. Loud talking, noisy movements, and similar disruptions are considered normal and appropriate outside the classroom. However, some students present more enduring and serious problems. About 15 per cent of boys and 5 percent of girls show moderate to severe adjustment problems.

Dealing with Offenders: Many teachers strike tacit bargains with persistent offenders, minimizing educational demands and even interactions with them in turn for a degree of compliance. Teachers often will not intervene with such students when their misbehaviour is relatively mild but they will over-react when they do intervene, these reinforcing students perceptions that the teacher in picking on them. In general, indirect methods that try to avoid dealing with problems or pretend that they do not exist are more likely to reinforce than to extinguish the problem behaviour. Although, it is true that teachers may have to spend a great deal of time working with them individually, the general principles of classroom management hold for disturbed students just as for other students.

4.8. Differential Teaching

There is a general tendency in some classrooms for low students to be treated in ways that differ from how students believed to be more capable are treated. Good and Brophy (1990) cites the general differences as presented below.

Students believed to be more capable have,

- More opportunity to perform publically on management tasks
- More autonomy (e.g., mere choice in assignment, fewer interruptions)
- More assignments that deal with comprehension, understanding

- More opportunity to think
- More opportunity for self-evaluation
- More honest/contingent feed back
- More respect for the learner as an individual with unique interests and needs.

As pointed out by many studies, differential teaching does not occur in all classrooms. Teachers differ considerably in how much they differentiate their treatment of students for whom they hold different expectations.

Sometimes the differences are due primarily to the students rather than to the teacher. If the students believed to be less capable seldom raise their hands, for example, it is difficult for the teacher to ensure that they get as many response opportunities as more capable students, and if their contributions are of lower quality, it is difficult for the teacher to use their ideas just as frequently.

Some forms of differential teaching may be appropriate at times and may even represent good individualized instruction rather than inappropriate projection of negative expectations. Although differential treatment of high and low achievers does not automatically indicate inappropriate teacher expectations or undesirable teacher-expectations effects, it is wise to keep these possibilities in mind when making instructional decisions and monitoring one's teaching. It is possible to improve the achievers progress of low achievers by changing teacher behaviour and to do so without adversely affecting their classmates.

4.9. Remedial Teaching

The simplest way to ensure that students expect success is to make sure that they achieve success consistently by beginning at their level, moving in small steps and preparing them sufficiently for each new step so that they can adjust to it without much confusion or frustration. Levels of success that students can achieve on a particular task depend not only on the difficulty of the task itself but also on the degree to which the teacher prepares them for the task through advance instruction and assists their learning efforts through guidance and feedback.

It can be difficult to program low achievers for success, especially in heterogeneous classrooms. The teacher can help the students by providing extra instruction and assistance and by monitoring their progress more frequently. If necessary, the teacher can divide the class into subgroups that receive differentiated instruction and assignments, and grade according to mastery learning procedures that do not penalize slower students for the extra time that they take to achieve mastery or according to criteria specified in individualized performance.

5
Different Approaches in Science Teaching

5.1. Enquiry and Discovery Approaches

Science is fundamentally concerned with exploring and interpreting the physical world through three fundamental disciplines, namely Physics, Chemistry and Biology. Science if studied properly, it develops the power of thinking and reasoning, curiosity, open mindedness and ultimately scientific temper. Science involves two components viz., content and process. So teaching of a particular content and process ha,s to be compatible with the 'nature of science'. A modern science teacher should be a stage setter and initiator of scientific thinking. Enquiry approach aims at encouraging the student to be inquisitive and curious-to ask and find solution of oneself.

Teaching science through enquiry approach leads to the unfolding of the child's mind. Enquiry supplements the existing set of knowledge. It leads students with added strength to face the challenges. The spirit of enquiry invokes joy, thrill and excitement. Instruction with enquiry approach begins with presentation of a puzzling event for which explanations are to be obtained. When the children are given the challenge to find out such explanation they may ask the teacher some questions for which readymade answers should not be given. They may be encouraged to enquire for themselves in the form of possible explanations to be verified. For verifying the acceptability of these explanations they may ask questions, for which the teacher should answer by saying only 'YES' or 'No'. Such interaction will help them formulate hypotheses. They verify these hypotheses after searching through references and doing small experiments. Thus, they are trained to learn on their own. As science is an ongoing process of enquiry, children should be made to learn science through that unique nature. Enquiry approach of teaching owes much to Joseph J. Schwab and Suchman.

In discovery approach of teaching science children are provided opportunities to solve scientific problems quite independently or through guided approach by which they are made to follow certain systematic steps. The students are often sent to the laboratory as researchers or investigators. The lesson starts with a problem. Students plan and carry out their own procedures to solve the problem. They collect and interpret data, formulate and test hypotheses, and draw their own conclusions. The teacher only guides and encourages. In discovery approach, children are engaged in the 'process of science'. Discovery approach owes much to the ideas of Amstrong, Bruner, Gagne and Piaget.

The most common limitation of Enquiry and Discovery approach is the time factor. The content covered may be very limited but the objectives of discovery approach are much broader. What is lost in terms of subject content may be gained in terms of the skill for science enquiry.

Expository approach- All cues are provided by the teacher
Teacher centered
Discovery approach - No cues are provided by the teacher
Pupil centered

5.2. Inductive and Deductive Approaches

Induction and deduction are two techniques of thinking and reasoning used for arriving generalizations or valid conclusions. These could be adopted for developing effective methods in teaching concepts, principles and processes in Science.

1. Inductive Thinking

In induction thinking moves from particular to general. By closely observing and interpreting a number of concrete examples, the students arrive at a generalization. In this method rules are discovered, by pupils themselves by studying enough number of examples. This approach is mainly developmental in nature. It gives opportunity for active participation by the student in the process of discovery. This reduces the dependence on memorization.

Merits

(a) The child develops independence and self confidence
(b) This is a psychological method
(c) It is a logical method
(d) It gives opportunity for active participation by students
(e) As the conclusions are made from concrete examples the generalization arrived at will be meaningful to the learner
(f) It reduces dependence on memorization and homework

Limitations

(a) It is laborious and time consuming
(b) It is not suitable for all topics
(c) Application of the generalizations is not attempted in inductive thinking
(d) The insufficient data any sometimes lead the learner to wrong generalization.

2. *Deductive Thinking*

In this procedure, thinking moves from the general to the particular; abstract to concrete. In this method the learner assumes a rule or generalization and apply it to interpret a particular situation or to further verify it is acceptability.

	Deductive Method	*Inductive Method*
1.	General to particular approach.	Particular to general approach.
2.	It is a method of verification.	It is a method of discovery.
3.	Very quick method as generalisations are accepted.	Very slow method as a new generalization.
4.	Encourages dependence on accepted principles.	Principles are independently generated.
5.	Learner gets ready made knowledge.	Learner gets first hand information.
6.	Downward movement.	Upward movement.

As methods of teaching, induction or deduction cannot be complete by itself. They have to supplement each other. To begin with, inductive thinking can be adopted, but when once a generalization is arrived at it has to be subjected to verification by deductive thinking. That is why in 'inductive-deductive approach' is considered as a complete method in the teaching of generalizations. Start with induction and end with deduction.

5.3. Conceptual vs. Factual Approach

Under the conceptual approach of teaching, concepts are given central position while facts are considered as secondary. For example while learning about respiration the central idea of that process is considered as crucial, while organs and modes of respiration considered secondary items that would support formulation of the main concept. It is humanly impossible to remember various facts pertaining to various scientific concepts and processes. If these facts are formed into concepts they can easily be remembered and applied. Hence conceptual approach is given priority by the modern educators. Concepts formation is a classification behaviour. It depends on the student's ability to observe a wide range of characteristics to be obeyed by all members of a category of objects or phenomena and there by develop a generalized notion in the form of a mental image representing a category as a whole, by abstracting these specific characteristics.

For example cow is an organism that delivers off springs and rears them by giving breast milk. This is true of a woman too. A she-bat also follows the same practice. These three organisms are entirely different in very many respects, but on the basis of the above two characteristics common to all the three, these can be brought under the same category leading to the concepts 'mammal'. This will economise effort and make knowledge systematic. Pupils can be made to attain such concepts through observation, analysis of attributes, comparison, classification, definition and verification. This approach can be qualified as the conceptual approach in teaching. This is very important in science because concepts form the vocabulary of the "language of science".

Approaching science through concepts makes science learning natural and simple. In factual approach of teaching science facts are considered central. Pupils have to apprehend and retain these facts. This approach is applicable when the children are having very little background knowledge required for assimilating and generalizing ideas to abstract concepts. Hence factual approach of teaching finds a place in lower classes.

5.4. Inter-disciplinary Approach (Correlation in Science)

One of the important aims of the educative process is to achieve a unification of knowledge pertaining to the various branches of learning. Students cannot continue to learn science in isolation as compartmentalized disciplines that have little relation to each other. Hence ideally, integrated knowledge has to be taught in schools instead of teaching isolated and narrowly specified subjects. But in the present context, all the different subjects cannot be taught as an integrated whole by a single teacher at the high school level. This is so because in this age of rapid knowledge explosion, one teacher cannot specialize in all branches of knowledge. Thus, the need for division arises which leads to what we call the disciplinary approach. Even when we adopt the disciplinary approach of teaching, the message of integration of the subjects can be attained by following an inter-disciplinary approach by which the various disciplines are meaningfully correlated.

Correlation implies the reciprocal among various subjects in the curriculum. This approach helps pupils obtain a coherent view of science by establishing numerous links between the various branches of knowledge. Correlation of different subjects is essential for checking artificiality of treatment and for achieving unity of knowledge. It makes learning easier, more interesting and natural and practically significant to life.

The concept of correlation is not at all new in the field of education. Comenius (1592-1671) emphasized the importance of correlation in teaching. He was of the opinion that nothing could be taught in isolation. Herbart also advocated inter-disciplinary approach of teaching. Pupil should get the impression that each subject supplements and complements others. They should also feel that the subject taught in schools have something to do with day-to-day life. In the Basic Education Scheme correlation with various branches of knowledge as well as with life occupies a pivotal position, and it is not the craft that makes the school Basic, but its correlation with various branches of knowledge as well as with life that makes it really Basic, Correlation or inter-disciplinary approach of science can be explained under three heads.

(i) Correlation of science subjects with one another.
(ii) Correlation of science with other school subjects.
(iii) Correlation of science with the social, physical environments.

Correlation of science may be either incidental or systematic. Incidental correlation is secured by coordinating each topic with all allied materials from other subjects. The success of such correlation depends on the wide knowledge and versatility of the teacher. Systematic correlation is achieved through a careful and purposeful reorganization of the curriculum in different subjects.

6
Innovative Practices

Some of the innovative practices in teaching and learning are detailed in this chapter.

6.1. Programmed Instruction

B.F. Skinner in 1958 devised a machine to increase the efficiency of teaching subjects like language, arithmetic and other important school subjects. The classroom teacher is impossible to concentrate in each and every child's daily progress in learning. This concept leads to discovery of teaching machine/auto instructional device and the theory which underlies this tool is known as programme instruction.

Objectives

1. The student will learn at his own pace.
2. The teacher may be free and concentrate on other important job (in framing, analyzing and evaluate the programme).
3. The student get training in self-evaluation, self improvement and then develops self confidence.
4. The teacher is able to place the materials to be learnt n more stepwise logical fashion catering to the need of the students.

Types of Programming

1) Linear or Extrinsic Type

This method emphasizes proceeding a straight line which means that each teacher has to pass through the same steps. It proceeds from one frame to another as decided by the programmer.

△ → △ → △ → △ → △
1 2 3 4 5

Sequence is determined by the programmer and learner has no option of his own in proceeding through sequence.

2) Branching or Intrinsic Style

This system offers a number of choices one of which is correct for a particular problem. It tells the student if he is wrong to go back to the original frame or to a sub-programme until he is correct.

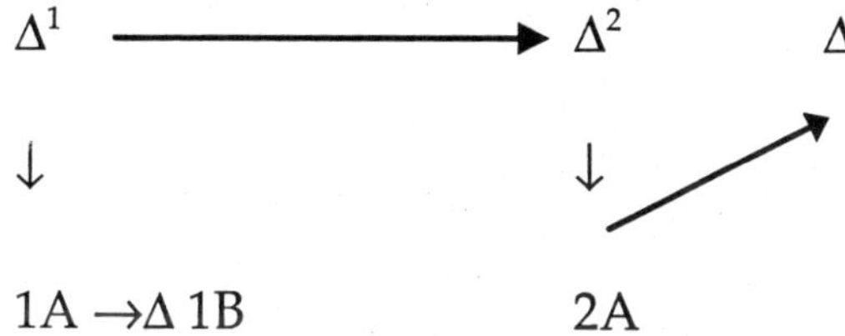

These are available in the form of a scrambled book. This book consists of pages which are not arranged sequentially. The students are given the matter to be learnt in small logical units and they are tested through multiple choice questions. If the responses are incorrect, they can go through a separate set of correctional materials.

6.2. Computer Assisted Instruction

Computer as a teaching machine has the advantage over all other kinds of educational technology in that it can provide a lot of flexibility in programme presentation and a number of students can work with it. Its print out can always help the learners to know where do they stand actually. With the help of computer language one can manipulate also large bodies data. It is a novel way for individualized instruction.

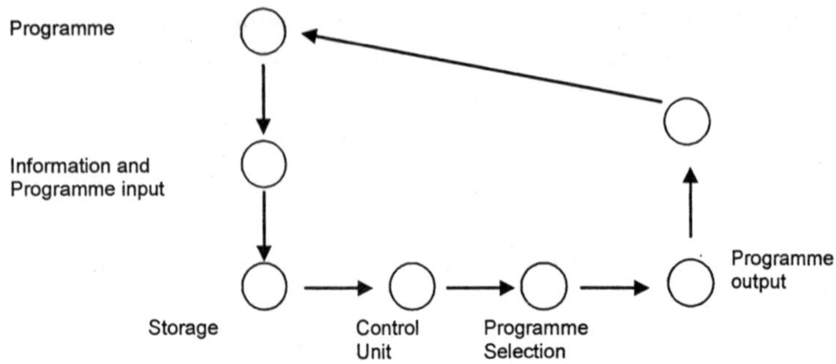

6.3. Mathetics

F. Gilbert in 1962 developed mathetics. According to him it is the systematic application of reinforcement theory to the analysis and reconstruction of those complex behavioural repertoires usually known as subject matter mastery, knowledge and skill.

In Greek 'Mathein' means to learn from which the word Mathematics is taken. In this approach the learner is shown the last step first in a sequence and then he works progressively backward to the first step. Secondly, it uses the largest units of which the learner is capable, on the argument that if the unit is too small, the inefficiency goes undetected. In contrast, both linear and branching programmes use small steps.

There are certain differences in these forms of programming but all of these have common base on a theory of –

STIMULUS (Information and Question)	→	RESPONSE (Reply)	→	FEEDBACK (Knowledge of Results)

6.4. Team Teaching

It is an innovation in educational practice in which two or more teachers teach a group of students. Team teaching is "a type of instructional organization, involving teaching personnels and the students discuss with them, in which two or more teachers are given responsibility of working together for all or significant part of the instruction of some group of students" – Shaplin.

According to Trump and Baynham, 'team teaching is an arrangement whereby two or more teachers, with or without teaching aids, co-operating plan, instruct and evaluate one or more class groups, in an appropriate instructional space and given length of time, so as to take advantage of the special competencies of the team members'

Team teaching is traditionally thought of as when more than one teacher is involved in instruction within a classroom. There are a few different models of team teaching, and more than one model may be carried out within one class period. There are many positive effects associated with team teaching, but there are also many things that need to be considered before jumping into a team teaching approach.

Significance

Higher expectations are placed on students and teachers of the 21st century than ever before. Different studies have been conducted that address different teaching methods for helping students meet these expectations. Team teaching is just one of the methods that has been explored. Additionally, as more attention is being brought to including special education students into the regular classroom, debates ensue about how that can be done effectively, presenting team teaching as the answer.

Types

- *Traditional team teaching* is a model in which two teachers within a classroom take equal responsibility for teaching the students and are actively involved at all times. One may be teaching while the other is writing notes on the board."
- *Supportive Instruction*" is a second model of team teaching in which one teacher teaches the material and the other teacher provides follow-up activities.
- "*Parallel Instruction*" is a form of team teaching in which students are split into two groups and each teacher is responsible for teaching his group.
- "*Differentiated Split Class*" team teaching involves splitting students into two groups based on achievement. One teacher provides remedial instruction to students who are

struggling on a skill while the other teacher provides enrichment to those who have grasped the skill.

- *The "Monitoring Teacher"* is another form of team teaching. In this model, one teacher assumes the role of instruction while the other teacher walks around the class and monitors students' behaviour and progress. Different types of team teaching may be used within one class period.

Use of Team Teaching

In view of the additional complexity which team teaching initiatives introduce into departmental organisation and in view of the time needed for staff to adapt to the new structures, it is relevant to ask what benefits accrue from team teaching. How, for instance, does team teaching benefit lecturers, part-time tutors, students, and departments as a whole?

- *For Lecturers,* who so often work alone, team teaching provides a supportive environment that overcomes the isolation of working in self-contained or departmentalized class-rooms. Being exposed to the subject expertise of colleagues, to open critique, to different styles of planning and organisation, as well as methods of class presentation, teachers can develop their approaches to teaching and acquire a greater depth of understanding of the subject matter of the unit or module.
- *Part-time staff* can be drawn more closely into the department as members of teams than is usually the case, with a resulting increase in integration of course objectives and approaches to teaching.
- *Team teaching can lead to better student performance* in terms of greater independence and assuming responsibility for learning. Exposure to views and skills of more than one teacher can develop a more mature understanding of knowledge often being problematic rather than right or wrong. Learning can become more active and involved. Students could eventually make an input into team planning.
- *Team teaching aids the professional and interpersonal dynamics of departments* leading to closer integration of staff.

Effects

When team teaching is organized and carried out effectively, positive effects are felt by students, parents and school faculty. Research shows that students taught using a team teaching approach have higher levels of achievement. There is also more contact with parents by teachers in a team teaching situation. Additionally, schools that employ team teaching have teachers who are more satisfied with their job, resulting in an improved work climate.

Team teaching involves a group of instructors working purposefully, regularly, and cooperatively to help a group of students of any age learn. Teachers together set goals for a course, design a syllabus, prepare individual lesson plans, teach students, and evaluate the results. They share insights, argue with one another, and perhaps even challenge students to decide which approach is better.

Teams can be single-discipline, interdisciplinary, or school-within-a-school teams that meet with a common set of students over an extended period of time. New teachers may be paired with veteran teachers. Innovations are encouraged, and modifications in class size, location, and time are permitted. Different personalities, voices, values, and approaches spark interest, keep attention, and prevent boredom.

The team-teaching approach allows for more interaction between teachers and students. Faculty evaluate students on their achievement of the learning goals; students evaluate faculty members on their teaching proficiency. Emphasis is on student and faculty growth, balancing initiative and shared responsibility, specialization and broadening horizons, the clear and interesting presentation of content and student development, democratic participation and common expectations, and cognitive, affective, and behavioral outcomes. This combination of analysis, synthesis, critical thinking, and practical applications can be done on all levels of education, from kindergarten through graduate school.

Working as a team, teachers model respect for differences, interdependence, and conflict-resolution skills. Team members together set the course goals and content, select common materials such as texts and films, and develop tests and final examinations for all students. They set the sequence of topics and supplemental materials. They also give their own interpretations of the materials and use their own teaching styles. The greater the agreement on common objectives and interests, the more likely that teaching will be interdependent and coordinated.

Teaching periods can be scheduled side by side or consecutively. For example, teachers of two similar classes may team up during the same or adjacent periods so that each teacher may focus on that phase of the course that he or she can best handle. Students can sometimes meet all together, sometimes in small groups supervised by individual teachers or teaching assistants, or they can work singly or together on projects in the library, laboratory, or fieldwork. Teachers can be at different sites, linked by video-conferencing, satellites, or the Internet.

Breaking out of the taken-for-granted single-subject, single-course, single-teacher pattern encourages other innovations and experiments. For example, students can be split along or across lines of sex, age, culture, or other interests, and then recombined to stimulate reflection. Remedial programs and honours sections provide other attractive opportunities to make available appropriate and effective curricula for students with special needs or interests. They can address different study skills and learning techniques. Team teaching can also offset the danger of imposing ideas, values, and mindsets on minorities or less powerful ethnic groups. Teachers of different backgrounds can culturally enrich one another and students.

Warrick has suggested four important approaches for organizing team teaching which purviews needs, age groups, subject content and available instructional materials.

a) Thematic Approach

'Theme' is important in this type. Around a central theme leading topics are arranged to make the whole content an integrated one.

b) Concurrent Theme

In this, themes from two or more different areas may go together linking one with another. Taking concepts from mathematics, related concepts in physics can be taught by linking each other. Some of the equipment/ content from chemistry/physics can be used for each other's effective understanding though courses will remain independent of each other.

c) Cumulative Sequence

This approach is suited for older children at the college level though no harm in using this for younger lot. The peculiarity of this approach is that no theme as such is being present at the beginning of the teaching but an attempt is made to make an overall pattern by linking the topics. It is based on an inductive approach.

d) The Concentric Pattern

It starts with a known subject quite well known to the student. From 'known to unknown', is the basic principle of this approach. The related topics lead to wider and unknown periphery slowly and logically.

Advantages

All students do not learn at the same rate. Periods of equal length are not appropriate for all the learning situations. Educators are no longer dealing primarily with top-down transmission of the tried and true by the mature and experienced teacher to the young, immature, and inexperienced pupil in the single-subject classroom. Schools are moving toward the inclusion of another whole dimension of learning: the lateral transmission to every sentient member of society of what has just been discovered, invented, created, manufactured, or marketed. For this, team members with different areas of expertise are invaluable.

Of course, team teaching is not the only answer to all problems plaguing teachers, students, and administrators. It requires planning, skilled management, willingness to risk change and even failure, humility, open-mindedness, imagination, and creativity. But the results are worth it.

Teamwork improves the quality of teaching as various experts approach the same topic from different angles: theory and practice, past and present, different genders or ethnic backgrounds. Teacher strengths are combined and weaknesses are remedied. Poor teachers can be observed, critiqued, and improved by the other team members in a nonthreatening, supportive context. The evaluation done by a team of teachers will be more insightful and balanced than the introspection and self-evaluation of an individual teacher.

Working in teams spreads responsibility, encourages creativity, deepens friendships, and builds community among teachers. Teachers complement one another. They share insights, propose new approaches, and challenge assumptions. They learn new perspectives and insights, techniques and values from watching one another. Students enter into conversations between them as they debate, disagree with premises or conclusions, raise new questions, and point out consequences. Contrasting viewpoints encourage more active class participation and independent thinking from students, especially if there is team balance for gender, race, culture, and age. Team teaching is particularly effective with older and underprepared students when it moves beyond communicating facts to tap into their life experience.

The team cuts teaching burdens and boosts morale. The presence of another teacher reduces student-teacher personality problems. In an emergency one team member can attend to the problem while the class goes on. Sharing in decision-making bolsters self-confidence. As teachers see the quality of teaching and learning improve, their self-esteem and happiness grow. This aids in recruiting and keeping faculty.

Disadvantages

Team teaching is not always successful. Some teachers are rigid personality types or may be wedded to a single method. Some simply dislike the other teachers on the team. Some do not want to risk humiliation and discouragement at possible failures. Some fear they will be expected to do more work for the same salary. Others are unwilling to share the spotlight or their pet ideas or to lose total control.

Team teaching makes more demands on time and energy. Members must arrange mutually agreeable times for planning and evaluation. Discussions can be draining and group decisions take longer. Rethinking the courses to accommodate the team-teaching method is often inconvenient.

Opposition may also come from students, parents, and administrators who may resist change of any sort. Some students flourish in a highly structured environment that favours repetition. Some are confused by conflicting opinions. Too much variety may hinder habit formation.

Salaries may have to reflect the additional responsibilities undertaken by team members. Team leaders may need some form of bonus. Such costs could be met by enlarging some class sizes. Non-professional staff members could take over some responsibilities.

Considering all the factors, no doubt team teaching enhances the quality of learning and it is definite that it will spread widely in the future.

6.5. Simulation

Basically a role-playing process through what one learns a number of social skills. The word simulation means to create the artificial environment or situations which provide artificial explanations to participants. Student teachers can teach their peers in simulated classrooms following up discussions and criticism of lessons.

It is experiencing the student teacher through artificial environments how to cope with various classroom situations.

Different Ways of Simulation

1. Incident processing
2. Case method
3. Role playing
4. Situational exercises
5. Behavioural and business games which are task oriented.

1) Incident Process

In this process, incident is described if possible with the help of a tape recorder or a video film. Then the participant are asked how they are going to handle the situation. In case of trainee teachers, they will initiate a discussion by raising questions and solving them by giving their own suggestions. It is in a way helping the trainee teachers to perceive alternative solutions.

2) Case Method

It is more or less like an incident but case is definitely more comprehensive and represents a total picture of a situation consisting of many aspects. This leads to excursing more of discovery power and needs a lot of teacher involvement. Its real objective is to see the participants as the decision makers.

Characteristically the case method helps the trainee teachers to handle higher level cognitive and affective objectives. Trainee should be able to analyze, infer, synthesize and evaluate.

3) Role Playing

It is often used in psychology practical classes and where the trainee teachers are asked to play the roles depicting a real situation in life. In methodology class, this can be used where the trainees will assume different roles to provide participatory questions where one of their friends may assume the role of teaching a position of a specific topic. How to handle the odd questions? How to handle the very intelligent question? How to tackle a different child? This type of skills are learnt well in role playing under the supervision of the method teacher.

4) Situational Exercises

How classroom teachers are going to tackle a number of situations, how are they going to take effective decisions are practiced through situational exercises. His behaviour either expressed verbally or written on a performa containing all the situations will be thrown to the class for a discussion. The discussion should lead to feedback so that the particular behaviour can be practiced again keeping in mind the suggestions.

5) Behavioural Business Games

It is quite customary in primary schools for teaching children arithmetic to take help of game where children play the market game of selling and buying. This method can be used very effectively for teaching elementary concepts in mathematics/ science.

Role of Methodology Teacher in Simulation

1. He should select the proper way of simulation for realization of the objects.
2. He should arrange/modify/innovate proper materials for the chosen method of simulation.
3. After observing the trainee teacher, discussions should be arranged for the feedback.
4. He should evaluate his own choice of method and modify it accordingly.

6.6. Micro-teaching

D.W. Allen (1966). Invented in the mid-1960s at Stanford University by Dr. Dwight Allen, micro-teaching has been used with success for several decades now, as a way to help teachers acquire new skills.

Definition

> "Microteaching is a scaled down teaching encounter in class size and time."

In the original process, a teacher was asked to prepare a short lesson (usually 20 minutes) for a small group of learners who may not have been her own students. This is be videotaped, using Video Recorder. After the lesson, the teacher, teaching colleagues, a master teacher and the students together view the videotape and comment on what they saw happening, referencing the teacher's learning objectives. Seeing the video and getting comments from colleagues and students teachers get an often intense "under the microscope" view of their teaching.

Micro lessons are great opportunities to present sample "snapshots" of what/how you teach and to get some feedback from colleagues about how it was received. It's a chance to try teaching strategies that the teacher may not use regularly. It's a good, safe time to experiment with something new and get feedback on technique.

Since its inception in 1963, microteaching has become an established teacher-training procedure in many universities and school districts. This training procedure is geared towards simplification of the complexities of the regular teaching-learning process. Class size, time, task, and content is scaled down to provide optimal training environments. The supervisor demonstrates the skill to be practiced. This may be live demonstration, or a video presentation of the skill. Then, the group members select a topic and prepare a lesson of five to ten minutes. The teacher trainee then has the opportunity to practice and evaluate her use of the skills. Practice takes the form of a ten-minute micro-teaching session in which five to ten pupils are involved.

Concept of Micro-teaching

Micro-teaching is a teacher training technique which helps the teacher trainee to master the teaching skills. It requires the teacher trainee

1. to teach a single concept of conten.
2. using a specified teaching skill.
3. for a short time.
4. to a very small member of pupils.

In this way the teacher trainee practices the teaching skill in terms of definable, observable, measurable and controllable form with repeated cycles till he attains mastery in the use of skill.

Characteristic of Microteaching

- Microteaching is a highly individualized training device.
- Microteaching is an experiment in the field of teacher education which has been incorporated in the practice teaching schedule.
- It is a student teaching skill training technique and not a teaching technique or method.
- Microteaching is micro in the sense that it scale down the complexities of real teaching.
- Practicing one skill at a time.
- Reducing the class size to 5–10 pupils.
- Reducing the duration of lesson to 5–10 minutes.
- Limiting the content to a single concept.
- Immediate feedback helps in improving, fixing and motivating learning.
- The student are providing immediate feedback in terms of peer group feedback, tape recorded/CCTV.
- Microteaching advocates the choice and practice of one skill at a time.

Steps of Micro-teaching

The Micro-teaching programme involves the following steps:

1. Particular skill to be practised is explained to the teacher trainees in terms of the purpose and components of the skill with suitable examples.
2. The teacher trainer gives the demonstration of the skill in Micro-teaching in simulated conditions to the teacher trainees.

3. The teacher trainee plans a short lesson plan on the basis of the demonstrated skill for his/her practice.
4. he teacher trainee teaches the lesson to a small group of pupils. His lesson is supervised by the supervisor and peers.
5. On the basis of the observation of a lesson, the supervisor gives feedback to the teacher trainee. The supervisor reinforces the instances of effective use of the skill and draws attention of the teacher trainee to the points where he could not do well.
6. In the light of the feed-back given by the supervisor, the teacher trainee replans the lesson plan in order to use the skill in more effective manner in the second trial.
7. The revised lesson is taught to another comparable group of pupils.
8. The supervisor observes the re-teach lesson and gives re-feed back to the teacher trainee with convincing arguments and reasons.
9. The 'teach – re-teach' cycle may be repeated several times till adequate mastery level is achieved.

Feedback in microteaching is critical for teacher-trainee improvement. It is the information that a student receives concerning his attempts to imitate certain patterns of teaching. The built-in feedback mechanism in micro-teaching acquaints the trainee with the success of his performance and enables him to evaluate and to improve his teaching behaviour. Electronic media gadgets that can be used to facilitate effective feedback is a vital aspect of micro-teaching

B.K. Passi has given the following list of Teaching Skills in his book "Becoming Better Teacher; Micro-teaching Approach":

1. Writing instructional objectives;
2. Introducing a lesson;
3. Fluency in questioning;
4. Probing questioning;
5. Explaining;
6. Illustrating with examples;
7. Stimulus variation;
8. Silence and non-verbal cues;

9. Reinforcement;
10. Increasing pupil participation;
11. Using black board;
12. Achieving Closure; and
13. Recognizing attending behaviour.

Specifications of the selected skills are given below

Sl. No.	*Skill*	*Components*
1.	Probing Questions	Prompting, seeking further information, redirection, focusing, increasing critical awareness.
2.	Explaining	Clarity, continuity, relevance to content using beginning and concluding statements, covering essential points.
3.	Illustrating with Examples	Simple, relevant and interesting examples appropriate media, use of inducts, deductive approach.
4.	Stimulus variation	Body movements, gestures, change in speech pattern, change in interaction style, pausing, focusing, oral-visual switching.
5.	Reinforcement	Use of praise words and statements, accepting and using pupils' idea, repeating and rephrasing, extra vertical cues, use of pleasant and approving gestures and expressions, writing pupils' answer on the black board.
6.	Recognizing attending behaviour	Call pupils by names, Make norms of classroom behaviour, attending behaviour reinforced, clarity of direction, check non-attending behaviour, keep pupils in Eye Span, check inappropriate behaviour immediately.
7.	Use of blackboard	Legible, neat and adequate with reference to content covered.
8	Fluency in questioning	Grammatical correctness, conciseness, relevancy, specificity.
9	Silence and non verbal cues	Silence, facial cues, head movements, body movements, hand movements.
10	Increasing pupil participation	Using stimulus variation, questions.
11	Achieving closure	Consolidation of major points, providing opportunities for pupils to apply present knowledge.
12	Writing instructional objectives	Well stated, specification of minimum expected level of performance, relevant to the content.
13	Stimulus variation	Movements, gestures, change i speech pattern., focusing, change in interaction style, pausing, oral visual switching.

Micro-teaching Cycle

The six steps generally involved in micro-teaching cycle are : Plan, Teach, Feedback, Re-plan, Re-teach and Re-feedback.

- *Plan:* This involves the selection of the topic and related content of such a nature in which the use of components of the skill under practice may be made easily and conveniently. The topic is analyzed into different activities of the teacher and the pupils. The activities are planned in such a logical sequence where maximum application of the components of a skill is possible.
- *Teach:* This involves the attempts of the teacher trainee to use the components of the skill in suitable situations coming up in the process of teaching-learning as per his/her planning of activities. If the situation is different and not as visualized in the planning of the activities, the teacher should modify his/her behaviour as per the demand of the situation in the class. He should have the courage and confidence to handle the situation arising in the class effectively.
- *Feedback:* This term refers to giving information to the teacher trainee about his performance. The information includes the points of strength as well as weakness relating to his/her performance. This helps the teacher trainee to improve upon his/her performance in the desired direction.
- *Re-plan:* The teacher trainee re- plans his lesson incorporating the points of strength and removing the points not skillfully handled during teaching in the previous attempt either on the same topic or on another topic suitable to the teacher trainee for improvement.
- *Re-teach:* This involves teaching to the same group of pupils if the topic is changed or to a different group of pupils if the topic is the same. This is done to remove boredom or monotony of the pupil. The teacher trainee teaches the class with renewed courage and confidence to perform better than the previous attempt.
- *Re-feedback:* This is the most important component of Micro-teaching for behaviour modification of teacher trainee in the desired direction in each and every skill practice.

There can be variations as per requirement of the objective of practice session. These steps are diagramatically represented in the following figure :

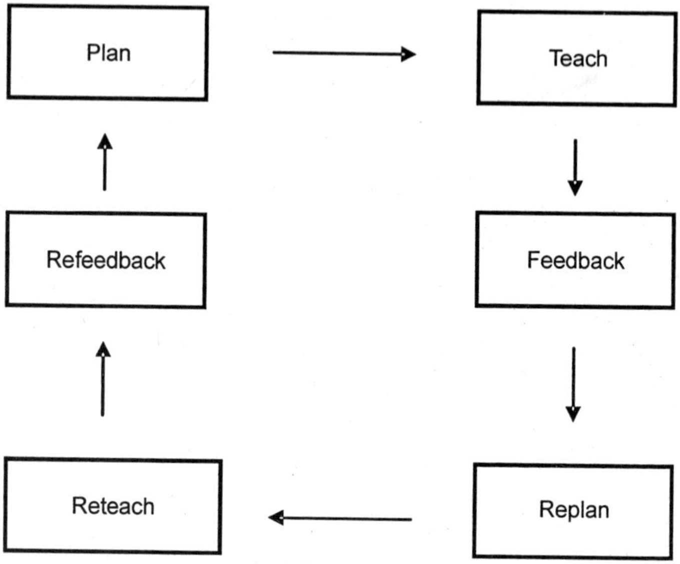

Link Practice (Integration of Teaching Skills)

When mastery has been attained in various skills, the teacher trainee is allowed to teach the skills together. This separate training programme to integrate various isolated skills is known as 'Link Practice'

It helps the trainee to transfer effectively all the skills learnt in the micro teaching sessions.

It helps to bridge the gap between training in isolated teaching skills and the real teaching situation faced by a student teacher.

7
Theories of Learning: Contribution to Science Education

Before discussing the theories contributing to science education, let us have an overview of the learning theories applicable to education in general.

7.1. Learning Theories – An Overview

This section examines twelve different theories on learning. They are listed below and explained further.

- Constructivism
- Behaviourism
- Piaget's Developmental Theory
- Neuroscience
- Brain-Based Learning
- Learning Styles
- Multiple Intelligences
- Right Brain/Left Brain Thinking
- Communities of Practice
- Control Theory
- Observational Learning and
- Vygotsky and Social Cognition.

Constructivism

Constructivism is a philosophy of learning founded on the premise that, by reflecting on our experiences, we construct our own understanding of the world we live in. Each of us generates our own "rules" and "mental models," which we use to make sense of our experiences. Learning, therefore, is simply the process of adjusting our mental models to accommodate new experiences.

Guiding Principles of Constructivism

- Learning is a search for meaning. Therefore, learning must start with the issues around which students are actively trying to construct meaning.
- Meaning requires understanding wholes as well as parts. And parts must be understood in the context of wholes. Therefore, the learning process focuses on primary concepts, not isolated facts.
- In order to teach well, we must understand the mental models that students use to perceive the world and the assumptions they make to support those models.
- The purpose of learning is for an individual to construct his or her own meaning, not just memorize the "right" answers and regurgitate someone else's meaning. Since education is inherently interdisciplinary, the only valuable way to measure learning is to make the assessment part of the learning process, ensuring it provides students with information on the quality of their learning.

Impact of Constructivism on Learning

Curriculum: Constructivism calls for the elimination of a standardized curriculum. Instead, it promotes using curricula customized to the students' prior knowledge. Also, it emphasizes hands-on problem solving.

Instruction: Under the theory of constructivism, educators focus on making connections between facts and fostering new understanding in students. Instructors tailor their teaching strategies to student responses and encourage students to analyze, interpret, and predict information. Teachers also rely heavily on open-ended questions and promote extensive dialogue among students.

Assessment: Constructivism calls for the elimination of grades and standardized testing. Instead, assessment becomes part of the learning process so that students play a larger role in judging their own progress.

Behaviourism

Behaviourism is a theory of human learning that only focuses on objectively observable behaviours and discounts mental activities. Behaviour theorists define learning as nothing more than the acquisition of new behaviour.

Experiments by behaviourists identify conditioning as a universal learning process. There are two different types of conditioning, each yielding a different behavioural pattern:

- Classic conditioning occurs when a natural reflex responds to a stimulus. The most popular example is Pavlov's observation that dogs salivate when they eat or even see food. Essentially, animals and people are biologically "wired" so that a certain stimulus will produce a specific response.
- Behavioural or operant conditioning occurs when a response to a stimulus is reinforced. Basically, operant conditioning is a simple feedback system: If a reward or reinforcement follows the response to a stimulus, then the response becomes more probable in the future. For example, leading behaviourist Skinner (Skinner, 1953) used reinforcement techniques to teach pigeons to dance and bowl a ball in a mini-alley.

There have been many criticisms of behaviourism. Behaviourism does not account for all kinds of learning, since it disregards the activities of the mind. Behaviourism does not explain some learning-such as the recognition of new language patterns by young children-for which there is no reinforcement mechanism. Research has shown that animals adapt their reinforced patterns to new information. For instance, a rat can shift its behaviour to respond to changes in the layout of a maze it had previously mastered through reinforcements.

Impact of Behaviourism on Learning

This theory is relatively simple to understand because it relies only on observable behaviour and describes several universal laws of behaviour. Its positive and negative reinforcement techniques can be very effective – both in animals, and in treatments for human disorders such as autism and antisocial behaviour. Behaviourism often is used by teachers, who reward or punish student behaviours.

7.2. Principles of Learning

Neuro-science

Neuroscience is the study of the human nervous system, the brain, and the biological basis of consciousness, perception, memory, and learning.

The nervous system and the brain are the physical foundation of the human learning process. Neuroscience links our observations about cognitive behaviour with the actual physical processes that support such behaviour. This theory is still "young" and is undergoing rapid, controversial development.

Some of the key findings of neuroscience are:

- The brain has a triad structure. Our brain actually contains three brains: the lower or reptilian brain that controls basic sensory motor functions; the mammalian or limbic brain that controls emotions, memory, and biorhythms; and the neocortex or thinking brain that controls cognition, reasoning, language, and higher intelligence.
- The brain is not a computer. The structure of the brain's neuron connections is loose, flexible, "webbed," overlapping, and redundant. It's impossible for such a system to function like a linear or parallel-processing computer. Instead, the brain is better described as a self-organizing system.
- The brain changes with use, throughout our lifetime. Mental concentration and effort alters the physical structure of the brain. Our nerve cells (neurons) are connected by branches called dendrites. There are about 10 billion neurons in the brain and about 1,000 trillion connections. The possible combinations of connections are about ten to the one-millionth power. As we use the brain, we strengthen certain patterns of connection, making each connection easier to create next time. This is how memory develops.

Neuroscience—Impact on Education

When educators take neuroscience into account, they organize a curriculum around real experiences and integrated, "whole" ideas. Plus, they focus on instruction that promotes complex thinking and the "growth" of the brain. Neuroscience proponents advocate continued learning and intellectual development throughout adulthood.

Brain-based Learning

This learning theory is based on the structure and function of the brain. As long as the brain is not prohibited from fulfilling its normal processes, learning will occur.

People often say that everyone can't learn. Yet the reality is that everyone does learn. Every person is born with a brain that functions as an immensely powerful processor. Traditional schooling, however, often inhibits learning by discouraging, ignoring, or punishing the brain's natural learning processes.

The core principles of brain-based learning state that:

- The brain is a parallel processor, meaning it can perform several activities at once, like tasting and smelling.
- Learning engages the whole physiology.
- The search for meaning is innate.
- The search for meaning comes through patterning.
- Emotions are critical to patterning.
- The brain processes wholes and parts simultaneously.
- Learning involves both focused attention and peripheral perception.
- Learning involves both conscious and unconscious processes.
- We have two types of memory: spatial and rote.
- We understand best when facts are embedded in natural, spatial memory.
- Learning is enhanced by challenge and inhibited by threat.
- Each brain is unique.

The three instructional techniques associated with brain-based learning are:

1. *Orchestrated immersion*: Creating learning environments that fully immerse students in an educational experience
2. *Relaxed alertness:* Trying to eliminate fear in learners, while maintaining a highly challenging environment
3. *Active processing:* Allowing the learner to consolidate and internalize information by actively processing it

Impacts on Education

- *Curriculum:* Teachers must design learning around student interests and make learning contextual.
- *Instruction:* Educators let students learn in teams and use peripheral learning. Teachers structure learning around real problems, encouraging students to also learn in settings outside the classroom and the school building.
- *Assessment:* Since all students are learning, their assessment should allow them to understand their own learning styles and preferences. This way, students monitor and enhance their own learning process.

How the brain works has a significant impact on what kinds of learning activities are most effective. Educators need to help students have appropriate experiences and capitalize on those experiences. As Renate Caine illustrates, three interactive elements are essential to this process:

- Teachers must immerse learners in complex, interactive experiences that are both rich and real. One excellent example is immersing students in a foreign culture to teach them a second language. Educators must take advantage of the brain's ability to parallel process.
- Students must have a personally meaningful challenge. Such challenges stimulate a student's mind to the desired state of alertness.
- In order for a student to gain insight about a problem, there must be intensive analysis of the different ways to approach it, and about learning in general. This is what's known as the "active processing of experience."

A few other tenets of brain-based learning are (1) Feedback is best when it comes from reality, rather than from an authority figure and (2) People learn best when solving realistic problems.

Designers of educational tools must be artistic in their creation of brain-friendly environments. Instructors need to realize that the best way to learn is not through lecture, but by participation in realistic environments that let learners try new things safely.

7.3. Learning Styles

This approach to learning emphasizes the fact that individuals perceive and process information in very different ways. The learning styles theory implies that how much individuals learn has more to do with whether the educational experience is geared toward their particular style of learning than whether or not they are "smart." In fact, educators should not ask, "Is this student smart?" but rather "How is this student smart?"

The concept of learning styles is rooted in the classification of psychological types. The learning styles theory is based on research demonstrating that, as the result of heredity, upbringing, and current environmental demands, different individuals have a tendency to both perceive and process information differently. The different ways of doing so are generally classified as:

- *Concrete and abstract perceivers:* Concrete perceivers absorb information through direct experience, by doing, acting, sensing, and feeling. Abstract perceivers, however, take in information through analysis, observation, and thinking.
- *Active and reflective processors:* Active processors make sense of an experience by immediately using the new information. Reflective processors make sense of an experience by reflecting on and thinking about it.

Traditional schooling tends to favour abstract perceiving and reflective processing. Other kinds of learning aren't rewarded and reflected in curriculum, instruction, and assessment nearly as much.

Learning Styles Theory – Impacts on Education

- *Curriculum:* Educators must place emphasis on intuition, feeling, sensing, and imagination, in addition to the traditional skills of analysis, reason, and sequential problem solving.

- *Instruction:* Teachers should design their instruction methods to connect with all four learning styles, using various combinations of experience, reflection, conceptualization, and experimentation. Instructors can introduce a wide variety of experiential elements into the classroom, such as sound, music, visuals, movement, experience, and even talking.
- *Assessment:* Teachers should employ a variety of assessment techniques, focusing on the development of "whole brain" capacity and each of the different learning styles.

Right Brain vs Left Brain

This theory of the structure and functions of the mind suggests that the two different sides of the brain control two different "modes" of thinking. It also suggests that each of us prefers one mode over the other.

Experimentation has shown that the two different sides, or hemispheres, of the brain are responsible for different manners of thinking. The following table illustrates the differences between left-brain and right-brain thinking:

Left Brain	Right Brain
Logical	Random
Sequential	Holistic
Rational	Intuitive
Analytical	Synthesizing
Objective	Subjective
Looks at parts	Looks at wholes

Most individuals have a distinct preference for one of these styles of thinking. Some, however, are more whole-brained and equally adept at both modes. In general, schools tend to favor left-brain modes of thinking, while downplaying the right-brain ones. Left-brain scholastic subjects focus on logical thinking, analysis, and accuracy. Right-brained subjects, on the other hand, focus on aesthetics, feeling, and creativity.

Impacts on Learning

- *Curriculum:* In order to be more "whole-brained" in their orientation, schools need to give equal weight to the arts, creativity, and the skills of imagination and synthesis.
- *Instruction*: To foster a more whole-brained scholastic experience, teachers should use instruction techniques that connect with both sides of the brain. They can increase their classroom's right-brain learning activities by incorporating more patterning, metaphors, analogies, role playing, visuals, and movement into their reading, calculation, and analytical activities.
- *Assessment:* For a more accurate whole-brained evaluation of student learning, educators must develop new forms of assessment that honour right-brained talents and skills.

7.4. Piaget's Theory and its Educational Implications

Swiss biologist and psychologist Jean Piaget (1896-1980) is renowned for constructing a highly influential model of child development and learning. Piaget's theory is based on the idea that the developing child builds cognitive structures–in other words, mental "maps," schemes, or networked concepts for understanding and responding to physical experiences within his or her environment. Piaget further attested that a child's cognitive structure increases in sophistication with development, moving from a few innate reflexes such as crying and sucking to highly complex mental activities.

His view of how children's mind works and develops has been enormously influential, particularly in educational theory. His particular insight was the role of maturation (simply growing up) in children's increasing capacity to understand their world: they cannot undertake certain tasks until they are psychologically mature enough to do so. His research has spawned a great deal more, much of which has undermined the detail of his own, but like many other original investigators, his importance comes from his overall vision.

He proposed that children's thinking does not develop entirely smoothly: instead, there are certain points at which it "takes off" and moves into completely new areas and capabilities. He saw these transitions as taking place at about 18 months, 7 years and

11 or 12 years. This has been taken to mean that before these ages children are not capable (no matter how bright) of understanding things in certain ways, and has been used as the basis for scheduling the school curriculum. Whether or not *should* be the case is a different matter.

Stages of Cognitive Development

Stage	*Characterised by*
Sensorimotor (Birth-2 yrs)	Differentiates self from objects. Recognizes self as agent of action and begins to act intentionally: e.g. pulls a string to set mobile in motion or shakes a rattle to make a noise. Achieves object permanence: realizes that things continue to exist even when no longer present to the sense.
Pre-operational (2-7 years)	Learns to use language and to represent objects by images and words. Thinking is still egocentric: has difficulty taking the viewpoint of others. Classifies objects by a single feature: e.g. groups together all the red blocks regardless of shape or all the square blocks regardless of colour.
Concrete operational (7-11 years)	Can think logically about objects and events. Achieves conservation of number (age 6), mass (age 7), and weight (age 9). Classifies objects according to several features and can order them in series along a single dimension such as size.
Formal operational (11 years and up)	Can think logically about abstract propositions and test hypotheses systematically. Becomes concerned with the hypothetical, the future, and ideological problems.

Piaget's Key Ideas

Adaptation What it says: adapting to the world through assimilation and accommodation.

Assimilation The process by which a person takes material into their mind from the environment, which may mean changing the evidence of their senses to make it fit.

Accommodation The difference made to one's mind or concepts by the process of assimilation.

Note that assimilation and accommodation go together: you can't have one without the other.

Classification	The ability to group objects together on the basis of common features.
Class Inclusion	The understanding, more advanced than simple classification, that some classes or sets of objects are also sub-sets of a larger class. (E.g. there is a class of objects called dogs. There is also a class called animals. But all dogs are also animals, so the class of animals includes that of dogs).
Conservation	The realisation that objects or sets of objects stay the same even when they are changed about or made to look different.
Decentration	The ability to move away from one system of classification to another one as appropriate.
Egocentrism	The belief that you are the centre of the universe and everything revolves around you: the corresponding inability to see the world as someone else does and adapt to it. Not moral "selfishness", just an early stage of psychological development.
Operation	The process of working something out in your head. Young children (in the sensorimotor and pre-operational stages) have to act, and try things out in the real world, to work things out (like count on fingers): older children and adults can do more in their heads.
Schema (or scheme)	The representation in the mind of a set of perceptions, ideas, and/or actions, which go together.
Stage	A period in a child's development in which he or she is capable of understanding some things but not others.

Piaget's theory identifies four developmental stages and the processes by which children progress through them. The four stages are:

1. *Sensorimotor stage (birth – 2 years old)*–The child, through physical interaction with his or her environment, builds a

set of concepts about reality and how it works. This is the stage where a child does not know that physical objects remain in existence even when out of sight (object permanance).

2. *Preoperational stage (ages 2-7)*–The child is not yet able to conceptualize abstractly and needs concrete physical situations.
3. *Concrete operations (ages 7-11)*–As physical experience accumulates, the child starts to conceptualize, creating logical structures that explain his or her physical experiences. Abstract problem solving is also possible at this stage. For example, arithmetic equations can be solved with numbers, not just with objects.
4. *Formal operations (beginning at ages 11-15)*–By this point, the child's cognitive structures are like those of an adult and include conceptual reasoning.

Educational Implications

Curriculum: Educators must plan a developmentally appropriate curriculum that enhances their students' logical and conceptual growth.

Instruction: Teachers must emphasize the critical role that experiences–or interactions with the surrounding environment–play in student learning. For example, instructors have to take into account the role that fundamental concepts, such as the permanence of objects, play in establishing cognitive structures.

7.5. Bruner's Theory: Learning by Discovery

Jerome S. Bruner was one of the 20th century's most influential educational psychologists. His idea of learning by discovery is very important in the area of science teaching. The essential criterion for discovery learning is that the learner organizes into final form the material to be learned. The procedure differs from reception learning in which teacher explains to the student all the information he must learn. Discovery learning is like wrapping your own package; reception learning is like having some open it for you.

Bruner set down some controversial statements about curriculum development. He said, "Any subject can be taught effectively in some intellectually honest form to any child at any stage of development".

The real issue is, how we can develop mere effective instructional programs for the young child. Bruner's answer is to co-ordinate the mode of presentation of the material to the way in which the child can learn it. The child progresses from sensory (*enactive*) representation to concrete (*iconic*) representation and, finally to abstract (*symbolic*) representation; the teaching sequence should be the same. Curriculum organization should be ordered so that the child first experiences the material, then reacts to a concrete presentation of it, and finally, symbolizes it.

Bruner said, "curriculum of a subject should be determined by the most fundamental understanding that can be achieved of underlying principles that give structure to that subject.

Bruner mentions that you must allow the student to become a problem solver, to function in the same way as a scientist, historian or mathematician. Let students discover meaning for themselves, and the teacher enables them to learn concepts in the language they understand.

Discovery learning leads to self reward because the learner achieves satisfaction from finding solutions to problems on his own and is less dependent on extrinsic rewards. By placing emphasis on discovery, student learns to organize problems rather than attacking these by using hit-and-miss methods. Second, intrinsic motivation is the alternative to extrinsic motivation. Third, a student who has practised discovery learning can apply the same skills and techniques to work through real problems in his environment.

Discovery learning is an inquiry-based, constructivist learning theory that takes place in problem solving situations where the learner draws on his or her own past experience and existing knowledge to discover facts and relationships and new truths to be learned. Students interact with the world by exploring and manipulating objects, wrestling with questions and controversies, or performing experiments. As a result, students may be more likely to remember concepts and knowledge discovered on their own (in contrast to a transmissionist model). Models that are based upon discovery learning model include: guided discovery, problem-based learning, simulation-based learning, case-based learning, incidental learning, among others.

Proponents of this theory believe that discovery learning has many advantages, including:

- encourages active engagement;
- promotes motivation;
- promotes autonomy, responsibility, independence;
- the development of creativity and problem solving skills; and
- a tailored learning experience .

Critics have sometimes cited disadvantages including:

- creation of cognitive overload,
- potential misconceptions,
- teachers may fail to detect problems and misconceptions.

Here, Bruner writes about the process of pedagogy. He describes the key instructional components of curriculum: its sequence of activities in which learners become self-sufficient problem-solvers:

Instruction consists of leading the learner through a sequence of statements and restatements of a problem or body of knowledge that increase the learner's ability to grasp, transform, and transfer what he is learning. In short, the sequence in which a learner encounters materials within a domain of knowledge affects the difficulty he will have in achieving mastery. If it is true that the usual course of intellectual development moves from enactive through iconic to symbolic representation of the world, it is likely that an optimum sequence will progress in the same direction.

Optimal sequences cannot be specified independently of the criterion in terms of which final learning is to be judged. A classification of such criteria will include at least the following: speed of learning; resistance to forgetting; transferability of what has been learned to new instances; form of representation in terms of which what has been learned in terms of cognitive strain imposed; effective power of what has been learned in terms of its generativeness of new hypotheses and combinations.

Instruction is a provisional state that has as its object to make the learner of problem-solver self-sufficient. The tutor must correct the learner in a fashion that eventually makes it possible for the learner to take over the corrective function himself. Otherwise the result of instruction is to create a form of mastery that is contingent upon the perpetual presence of the teacher.

Bruner's Theory of Instruction indicates the following 4 elements :

1. *Readiness*: Learners should have a pre-disposition to learning. Readiness is promoted through motivation. The most effective motivation is problem solving. Problem solving arouses curiosity (arrival activities – asking, not telling).
2. *Structure*: The content must be structured so that learners understand it (delivery).

The content should be represented in 3 ways:
- (i) Enactive representation (demos);
- (ii) Iconic representation (images); and
- (iii) Symbolic representation (symbols)

3. *Sequence:* Material must be presented in a sequence giving the learners the opportunity to acquire, transform and transfer learning (objectives).
4. *Curriculum*: Learners re-visit ideas and concepts over a period of time but at increasingly complex levels. (Teaching and Learning strategies).

So an important educational practice described by Bruner is the spiral curriculum, which develops and re-develops topics at different grades. Once a child has learned something at simplified levels, he returns to the topic at a more advanced level. The basic principles of a discipline are studied over and over again at different grade levels, but at higher levels of complexity.

7.6. Gagne's Learning Theory

One of the important issues in learning involves the answer to the question, "when is the student ready to learn?" Gagne attributes differences in developmental readiness to previously learned intellectual skills. If a child cannot solve a particular task the chances are that he has not acquired the pre-requisite or subordinate skills related to the task. The child can learn any task if he acquires the intellectual skills that are pre-requisites.

During the 1960s (Anglin, 1991), there was a flurry of activity within the field of instructional development that focused on *systems* of instruction. It was during this time that the components of the instructional system and their system properties were articulated. In 1965 Robert Gagne published his book entitled *The Conditions of Learning*. In his book, Gagne (1965) described the analysis of learning objectives, and how these different classes of learning objectives relate to the appropriate instructional designs.

Gagne (1985), distinguishes between two types of conditions, internal and external. The internal conditions can be described as "states" and include attention, motivation and recall. The external conditions can be thought of as factors surrounding one's behavior, and include the arrangement and timing of stimulus events. Thus, his phases of learning include:

- Phase I: receiving the stimulus situation
- Phase II: stage of acquisition
- Phase III: storage
- Phase IV: retrieval

Implications for Instructional Technology

Gagne's (1965) theory of conditions of learning has several implications for instructional technology. The design of instruction should involve: analyzing requirements, selecting media and designing the instructional events. Additionally the instructional technologist must keep in mind the following learning concepts when developing methods of instruction.

- Skills should be learned on at a time and each new skill learned should build on previously acquired skills.
- The analysis phase must identify and describe the prerequisite lower level skills and knowledge required for an instructional objective.
- Lower level objectives must be mastered before higher level ones.
- Objectives must be stipulated in concrete behavioral terms.
- Positive reinforcement should be used in a repetitive manner.

Gagne's (1965) work has made significant contributions to the scientific knowledge base in the field of instructional technology particularly in the area of instructional design. He outlined several steps that should be used to plan and design instruction; these include:

- Identify the types of learning outcomes.
- Each outcome may have prerequisite knowledge or skills that must be identified.
- Identify the internal conditions or processes the learner must have to achieve the outcomes.
- Identify the external conditions or instruction needed to achieve the outcomes.
- Specify the learning context.
- Record the characteristics of the learners.
- Select the media for instruction.
- Plan to motive the learners.
- The instruction is tested with learners in the form of formative evaluation.
- After the instruction has been used, summative evaluation is used to judge the effectiveness of the instruction.

Gagne, feels that the child can acquire the sub skills that are related to the problem and then perform the task. The classification of these skills yields a learning hierarchy. This hierarchy identifies all the skills (mostly in the form of rules).

The Conditions of Learning

Rules: A defined concept is a particular kind of rule, a rule that classifies. A rule must be an internal state which governs one's behaviour, and enables one to demonstrate a relationship. A rule must be more than the verbal statement by which it is represented, for instance, the proposition "things equal to the same things are equal to each other".

Examples of Rule Learning

A young child may be told "Round things roll". Such a statement represents two different concepts, one the round things and second the rolling. If learning this rule is expected, the child must already know the concepts of 'round things' and 'roll'. If the concept 'round' has not already been acquired, the child may end up learning a more restricted rule, such as 'Balls roll'. If the rule is to be acquired in its fullest sense, the learner must know the concept 'round' in its full sense.

Learning Hierarchy

Most rules are not learned in isolation. The school student or an adult typically learns related sets of rules pertaining to a larger topic. The individual rules may have related to each other in the logical sense and also in psychological sense that the learning of some are pre-requisite to the learning of others, just as concepts are pre requisite to the learning of rules.

The psychological organization of intellectual skills may be represented as a learning hierarchy, often composed largely of rules. Two or more concepts may be pre-requisite to the learning of a single rule. Once a rule is learnt, it may combined with another rule and so on. The entire set of rules, organized in this way form a learning hierarchy.

An example of such a learning hierarchy is shown in the Figure. The intellectual skill of demonstrating the calculation of horizontal and vertical components of forces using vector diagrams is seen to depend on the pre-requisite learning of several sub-ordinate rules. In order to acquire the target skill the student must previously have learned to (1) use rules to verify the conditions of equilibrium, (2) represent the magnitude and directions of factor or parts of triangles and (3) employ trigonometric rules to represent the relationships in a right triangle (sine, cosine, tangent, etc.). If these three sets of sub-ordinates rules have been learned and can be made accessible in the learner's working memory, the learning of the tangent skill can proceed without a hitch. If these sub-ordinate rules are not known, learning of the target skill, is not possible.

Vector Resolution of Forces

Each of subordinate rules may be analyzed to reveal other subordinate rules or concepts which are pre-requisites to its learning, for example the skill of representing magnitudes and directions of forces as figure shows.

Many other topics learned in school have the character of organized sets of intellectual skills, and may be represented as learning hierarchies.

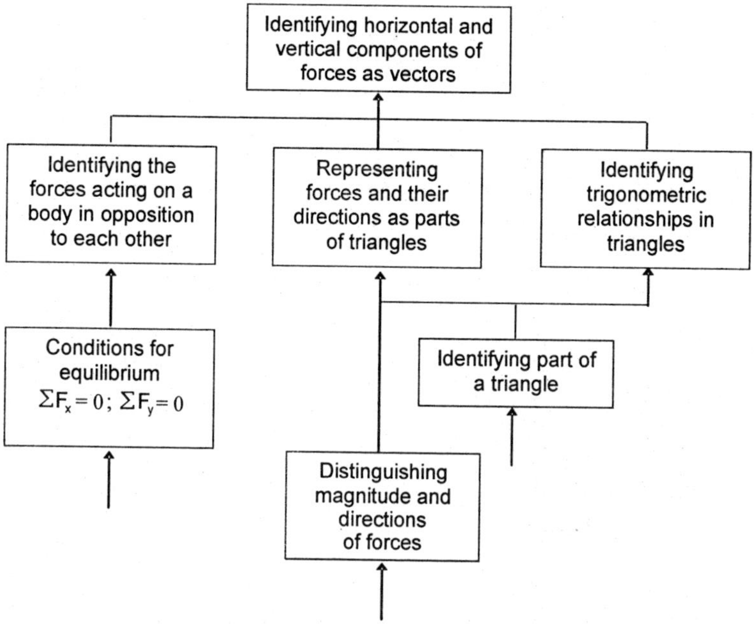

Fig. 7.1. A learning hierarchy showing the analysis of a rule to be learned (Dembo, 1977)

Educational Implications

The learning of rules is obviously of vast educational importance, because of the fact that rules make up the bulk of what is learned in the school. Another distinction of great relevance to education, emphasized, is that between rule and the verbal representation of the rule. However, the important role of verbal statements in the learning of new rules must be recognized. Much adult learning is accomplished by reading printed verbal statements. Such verbal statements communicate the to-be-learning rule and often constitute the first step in its learning, particularly when the component concepts have previously been learned.

7.7. Ausubel's Theory: Expository Teaching

David Ausubel was an American psychologist who did his undergraduate work at the University of Pennsylvania (pre-med and psychology). He was influenced by the work of Piaget. He served on the faculty at several universities and retired from academic life in 1973 and began his practice in psychiatry. Dr. Ausubel published several textbooks in developmental and educational psychology, and more than 150 journal articles. He was awarded the Thorndike Award for "Distinguished Psychological Contributions to Education" by the American Psychological Association (1976).

Theory

David Ausubel is a cognitive psychologist who favored expository teaching and its correlative- reception learning. In this type of teaching and learning, all the information to be learned is presented to the learner in its final form.

Ausubel, whose theories are particularly relevant for educators, considered neo-behaviorist views inadequate. Although he recognized other forms of learning, his work focused on verbal learning. He dealt with the nature of meaning, and believed the external world acquires meaning only as it is converted into the content of consciousness by the learner.

Meaningful Verbal Learning

Meaning is created through some form of representational equivalence between language (symbols) and mental context. Two processes are involved:

1. Reception, which is employed in meaningful verbal learning, and
2. Discovery, which is involved in concept formation and problem solving.

Ausubel's work has frequently been compared with Bruner's. The two held similar views about the hierarchical nature of knowledge, but Bruner was strongly oriented toward discovery processes, where Ausubel gave more emphasis to the verbal learning methods of speech, reading and writing.

Subsumption Theory

To subsume is to incorporate new material into one's cognitive structures. From Ausubel's perspective, this is the meaning of learning. When information is subsumed into the learner's cognitive structure it is organized hierarchically. New material can be subsumed in two different ways, and for both of these, no meaningful learning takes place unless a stable cognitive structure exists. This existing structure provides a framework into which the new learning is related, hierarchically, to the previous information or concepts in the individual's cognitive structure.

When one encounters completely new unfamiliar material, then rote learning, as opposed to meaningful learning, takes place. This rote learning may eventually contribute to the construction of a new cognitive structure which can later be used in meaningful learning. The two types of subsumption are:

1. Correlative subsumption – new material is an extension or elaboration of what is already known.
2. Derivative subsumption – new material or relationships can be derived from the existing structure. Information can be moved in the hierarchy, or linked to other concepts or information to create new interpretations or meaning. From this type of subsumption, completely new concepts can emerge, and previous concepts can be changed or expanded to include more of the previously existing information. This is "figuring out".

Ausubel is a proponent of didactic, expository teaching methods. From this perspective, expository (verbal) learning approaches encourage rapid learning and retention, whereas discovery learning (Bruner) facilitates transfer to other contexts.

Advance Organizers

Ausubel contributed much to the theoretical body of cognitive learning theory, but not as much to the practical classroom aspects as Bruner and others. Ausubel's most notable contribution for classroom application was the advance organizer.

The advance organizer is a tool or a mental learning aid to help students 'integrate new information with their existing knowledge, leading to "meaningful learning" as opposed to rote memorization. It is a means of preparing the learner's cognitive structure for the learning experience about to take place. It is a device to activate the relevant schema or conceptual patterns so that new information can be more readily 'subsumed' into the learner's existing cognitive structures.

Ausubel believed that it was important for teachers to provide a preview of information to be learned. Teachers could do this by providing a brief introduction about the way that information that is going to be presented is structured. This would enable students to start with a "Big Picture" of the upcoming content, and link new ideas, concepts, vocabulary, to existing mental maps of the content area.

Ausubel breaks down each academic subject into concepts that are hierarchically arranged. At the top of the discipline are the most broad or inclusive concepts, under which are subsumed the less inclusive concepts. Ausubel analogizes the organization of a learner's cognitive structure along similar lines.

Ausubel offers a number of organizational principles to help ensure meaningful learning. One is the process of *progressive differentiation*. Both the subject matter and cognitive structure are arranged similarly using this strategy, you teach the most general, inclusive concepts, first the less inclusive concepts second, and only after this do you teach specific information. The main advantage of progressive differentiation is the ease of assimilation and retention of new information for the student.

Another principle governing the organization of content in a field is *integrative reconciliation*. Ideas must be integrated and reconciled with previously learned ideas in a course. Ausubel contends that textbook authors compartmentalize knowledge into separate homogenous chapters in which they represent concepts in only one chapter and do not relate them to other ideas presented earlier or later in the course. Books written in this manner make it difficult for the student to explore the similarities and differences between ideas presented throughout the book.

The lack of integrative reconciliation in the organization of instructional material creates problems. First, since most authors and lecturers use multiple terms to represent the same concept, the confusion that results encourages rote learning. Second, artificial barriers are erected between the course content and the student who fails to see important relationship in the material.

Another way to aid the learning process is by the use of advance organizers, in the form of introductory materials presented in advance of the learning itself but presented at a higher level of abstraction and generally. The organizer provides sub-concepts that are reference points to aid the learner in subsuming the new material. One of the conditions for meaningful learning is that the learners possess relevant ideas in his cognitive structure to which he can relate_to the new material. An advance organizer serves this function.

The organizer can be a statement, a descriptive paragraph, a question, a demonstration, or even a film. It might be one section or it might be an entire lesson which proceeds the other lessons in a unit of work. The form of the organizer is less important than the fact that its solution must be clearly understood and continuously related to the material it is organizing.

The instructor can use organizers at many stages throughout the lesson or unit. As the learner moves to new material, new organizers provide a framework for relating new ideas to information already studied. Before students begin studying caste system in India, a brief presentation of social stratification as an organizer will help them understand the nature and purpose of the caste system. In mathematics, teaching the number line before proceeding to the addition and subtraction of negative members in another example of the effective use of an organizer.

7.8. Vygotsky and Social Cognition

The social cognition learning model asserts that culture is the prime determinant of individual development. Humans are the only species to have created culture, and every human child develops in the context of a culture. Therefore, a child's learning development is affected in ways large and small by the culture-including the culture of family environment-in which he or she is enmeshed.

Culture makes two sorts of contributions to a child's intellectual development. First, through culture children acquire much of the content of their thinking, that is, their knowledge. Second, the surrounding culture provides a child with the processes or means of their thinking, what Vygotskians call the tools of intellectual adaptation. In short, according to the social cognition learning model, culture teaches children both what to think and how to think.

Cognitive development results from a dialectical process whereby a child learns through problem-solving experiences shared with someone else, usually a parent or teacher but sometimes a sibling or peer.

Initially, the person interacting with child assumes most of the responsibility for guiding the problem solving, but gradually this responsibility transfers to the child.

Language is a primary form of interaction through which adults transmit to the child the rich body of knowledge that exists in the culture.

As learning progresses, the child's own language comes to serve as her primary tool of intellectual adaptation. Eventually, children can use internal language to direct their own behaviour.

Internalization refers to the process of learning-and thereby internalizing-a rich body of knowledge and tools of thought that first exist outside the child. This happens primarily through language.

A difference exists between what child can do on her own and what the child can do with help. Vygotskians call this difference the *zone of proximal development(zpd).*

Since much of what a child learns comes from the culture around her and much of the child's problem solving is mediated through an adult's help, it is wrong to focus on a child in isolation. Such focus does not reveal the processes by which children acquire new skills.

Interactions with surrounding culture and social agents, such as parents and more competent peers, contribute significantly to a child's intellectual development.

Vygotsky's Theory – Impacts on Learning

- *Curriculum*: Since children learn much through interaction, curricula should be designed to emphasize interaction between learners and learning tasks.
- *Instruction*: With appropriate adult help, children can often perform tasks that they are incapable of completing on their own. With this in mind, scaffolding-where the adult continually adjusts the level of his or her help in response to the child's level of performance-is an effective form of teaching. Scaffolding not only produces immediate results,

but also instills the skills necessary for independent problem solving in the future.

- *Assessment*: Assessment methods must take into account the zone of proximal development. What children can do of their own is their level of actual development and what they can do with the help is their level of potential development. Two children might have the same level of actual development, but given the appropriate help from an adult, one might be able to solve many more problems than the other. Assessment methods must target both the level of actual development and the level of potential development.

8
Curriculum Organization

The term curriculum comes from Latin word "currere" which means to run. "Curriculum is a runway of course through which one runs to reach a certain goal. According to Munoroe, "curriculum embodies all the experiences which are utilized by the school to attain the aim of education".

8.1. Definition

According to Cunningham, "Curriculum is the tool in the hands of an artist (teacher) to mould his materials (pupil) according to his ideals (aims and objectives) in his studio (school)."

As per Johnson (1967) "curriculum is a structured series of intended learning outcomes".

The traditional concept of curriculum as a list of lessons and topics which are expected to be covered in a specified period of time in class, has undergone in modern times.

Now the curriculum refers to the totality of experience that a child receive through various classroom activities as also from the activities in library, laboratory, workshop, assembly hall, play fields etc. Thus, in modern concept curriculum includes the whole life of school.

Science Curriculum: It is a part of general curriculum and it plays an important role in the development of innate potentialities of the child. From NCERT materials, the curriculum seems to be a package of some instructional material like syllabus, textbooks, teachers guides, kits guides, test items, slid type programmes and films for teacher training. But curriculum generally stands for:

(i) a school's written course of study and other course materials,
(ii) the subject content taught to the students,
(iii) the courses offered in a school, and
(iv) the total of planned learning experiences offered to students in a school.

A comprehensive definition

Curriculum is the planned and guided learning experience and intended outcomes, formulated through systematic reconstruction of knowledge and experience under the auspices of the school, for the learner's continuous and wilful growth in personal social competence. Curriculum is thus the sum total of all the experience which have to be provided for the good of the individual and the society.

Though curriculum is the core of the whole educational enterprise, it is influenced by other aspects of education and these factors should be considered while organizing the curriculum. The following are the factors contributing to curriculum organization:

1. Pupils;
2. Teacher;
3. Text book, instructional materials;
4. Examination and Evaluation;
5. Guidance and Counselling;
6. Supervision and Administration; and
7. Research.

8.2. Concept of Curriculum Organization

Sequential models of the curriculum process developed by Wheeler.

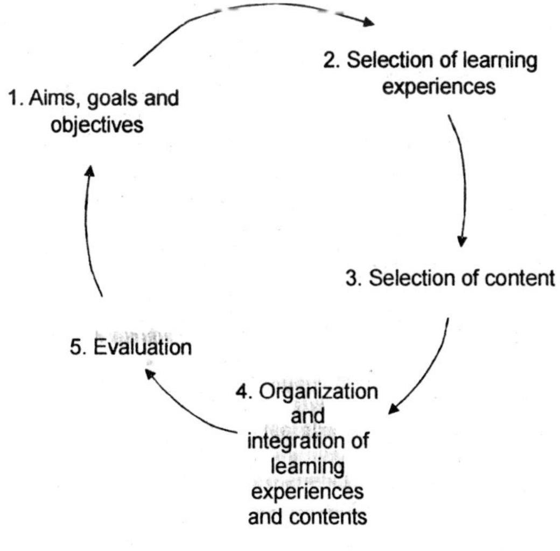

Criteria for Science Curriculum Organization

1. Meaningful and purposeful learning experience should be provided for students.
2. Learning styles of students should be considered carefully.
3. Teaching styles of teachers should be considered.
4. Learning expenses should be interesting to the students
5. Provision for diverse achievement levels should be there.

Functions of Science Curriculum Organization

1. To provide pupils continuous and sequential experience from the beginning to higher studies.
2. To approach science conceptually rather than factually.
3. To use those methods of instruction which familiarize students with the process of science.
4. To provide effectively for individual difference, ability, needs and interests.

Change in science education make changes in not only in the curriculum and organization but a change in the entire philosophy about the purpose and values of an education in the sciences. There is a renewed interest in how learning can be imported and made more effective. The shifting emphasizes in science by over the past decades are the following:

From	*To*
1. The product aspect of science	1. Process aspect
2. Role by and memorization	2. Concept formation and systematic thinking
3. The opinion that by has occurred if information can be repeated	3. The opinion that by has occurred if the pupil can use his knowledge in an explanatory or interpretive manner
4. Laboratory exercises to demonstrate, visualize or very known information	4. Laboratory experiments to raise problems, test inquiry skills and provide 'discovery' opportunities.
5. Education focused upon the world as it is today	5. Education for change and the future
6. Curriculum improvement through revision and experiment.	6. Curriculum improvement reform and innovation.
7. Instruction as information giving	7. Instruction as information processing

Philosophy of science curriculum can evolve only from an understanding of nature of science, Inquiry skills and scientific methods are supposed to reflect the nature of science as a process. The philosophy of science curriculum is concerned with four basic questions:

1. What characteristics distinguish scientific inquiry form other type of investigation?
2. What procedures should scientists follow?
3. What conditions must be satisfied for a scientific explanation to be correct?
4. What are the cognitive studies of scientific laws and principles?

Principles of Curriculum Organization

1. Principles of child centeredness: based on the child's needs and circumstances,
2. Principles of community centeredness: It should be able to serve the needs of community.
3. Principles of totality of experiences in the school, but not a set of subjects.
4. Principles of integration: (a) should integrate child's activity and the need of the society. (b) should integrate various meaningful one.
5. Principles of conservation: preservation and transfer of tradition on which civilization depends.
6. Principles of activity centeredness
7. Principles of elasticity and variety. Should not be rigid and should be changeable to suite the needs of society.
8. Curriculum should be dynamic and not stake.
9. Forward looking principles: It should help the child in principled utility, adjustment and prepare him for full and effective adult life.
10. Principle of creativity: Should place the pupil in the place of discoverer and provision should be made for creative type of activities.

8.3. Factors Affecting Curriculum Organization

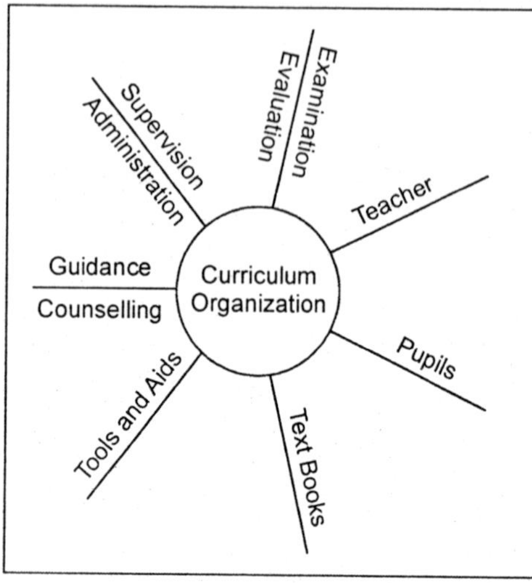

OTHER FACTORS:

1. Scientific Knowledge
2. Society Needs
3. Age Level of Student
4. Teacher
5. Text Books
6. Pupils
7. Tools and aids

Figure given above illustrates the factors affecting curriculum organization. Scientific Knowledge, Society Needs, Age Level of Student, Teacher, Text Books, Pupils and Tools and aids are the main factors affecting curriculum organization.

Organizing the Courses

This deals with the selection and planning of learning experiences, techniques and methods of teaching to be adopted, teaching facilities and teaching materials required etc.

After topics have been selected according to the relevant fundamental principles described above, they have to be systematically arranged so as to facilitate meaningful and effective transaction. The content should be arranged in a systematic manner. Here follows a discussion of the various methods of organizing and arranging the curriculum.

a) Concentric and Spiral Approaches

The whole curriculum is spread over a number of years. A general treatment of almost all topics are attempted at the beginning and it is developed in successive years according to the mental development of the pupils. In the beginning of the course, the whole aspect is given to pupils in a simplified way. In the next year more and more details of its parts are added. It follows the maxims of teaching, such as from whole to part, simple to complex, easy to difficult, etc. Bruner is the main exponent of this approach as he thinks that discovery learning is possible only if this approach is maintained. Sometimes this approach is referred to as *concentric* approach. But the term 'spiral approach' is preferred to the other. The term *spiral* gives the additional implication that while attempting graduation the linkage too is taken care of and the continuity of the topic concerned is never broken but while conceiving it as concentric only the widening of the scope is indicated but the linkage is not taken care of.

The arrangement of subject matter based on the principles of psychology is known as psychological approach. In this approach, the criterion for inclusion of an item in the curriculum will be the psychological needs, requirements, potentials, capacities, etc. appropriate for the developmental level of the stage for which the curriculum is being designed. In other words this approach is in turn with the principle of child-centeredness. In the logical approach stress is given to the logical sequencing of the subject concerned. Contents of every subject have been developed in tune with such a logical sequence. It is often criticized that by splitting topics to suit the developmental status of the learner, this logical development is broken. Logical approach demands maintaining the logical sequence while developing a curriculum. At the same time, a good curriculum, if carefully developed can maintain the psychological approach without sacrificing the logical sequencing of the subject. The only thing is that the logical continuity is taken care of at every stage of curriculum transaction done in tune with the psychological approach.

b) Topological and Unit Approaches

Every subject of study involves a number of topics. A topic is a comprehensive collection of related learning materials pertaining to specific area of the subject, systematically and sequentially arranged so as to get a holistic picture of those aspects. There are a large number of concepts, principles, processes, and skills associated with this area, which act as related parts of a 'whole'. Since these aspects are interrelated and maintain certain logical sequences and correlations, it is often advised that the topic should be thoroughly dealt with and mastered before passing on to another topic. This is known as the *topical approach in curriculum*. A topic may be so complex and might include a large number of items of varied difficulty, it is advisable not to cover all at the very first instance. A *spiral approach* may be adopted and study of the topic may be distributed over a distributed time span. For this, the topic may be divided into a number of units. Though a unit may be only part of the same topic it can be given a holistic unity by property linking the closely-knit ideals involved. Taking fundamental units of the topic first and then gradually taking other units one by one in due course will make learning more psychological and hence sound. This approach in curriculum planning is said to be '*unit approach*'.

Generally speaking, when a topic is complex and very large and involve units posing varied levels of difficulty it will be advisable to have the unit approach. Only thing is that care should be taken to effectively link all the units of the same topic as and when opportunities arise.

c) Topical Approach

In this, topics from a particular subject are selected and arranged in an order. Such topics are identified from the textbooks of higher classes.

For example: Super conductivity → identified from the social context.

d) Logical and Psychological Approach

Sequential arrangement of the topics of the syllabus based upon some logical approach and when the sequential order is based upon psychological principles of learning and teaching-psychological approach.

e) Subject Centred/Discipline-centred Approach (Popular Approach)

PSSC and Chemistry study projects are developed on discipline created approach syllabus was organized around certain conceptual scheme which represent inter-related concepts- Also known as conceptual approach. These approaches were based on the following assumptions. (1) Learners will learn concepts and will understand the structure of science, (2) The methodology of science or inquiry approach will be the method to acquire concepts.

f) Activity-Centred Approach

It is based on the principle that students will learn better if they are engaged in learning through some activities.

For example: Basic Education, in U.S.A., Science-A process approach.

In this approach transfer of learning becomes very effective. But this approach needs well-equipped laboratory.

g) The Environment-Based Approach

In this, content is directly related to the environment, which is drawn from physical, natural, social, political and cultural context.

h) Integrated Approach/Inter-Disciplinary Approach

Common concepts of different subjects are selected with a view to develop an awareness of the problems in society and to concentrate on the development of problem solving abilities. It includes learning activities from several of the specialized sciences, including behavioural science.

8.4. Organizing the Material

There are several forms for organizing the science materials in the science course like concentric topic method, historical method approach, nature study, nature rambling, type study, etc.

(a) *Concentric Method*: The whole science course is spared over a number of years. A general treatment of almost all topics is attempted at the beginning and it is developed in successive years according to the mental development of pupils. The method of arranging the course based on the maxim of teaching – from whole to part and from simple to complex. The method is advantageous as is revisiting what they learnt in previous years.

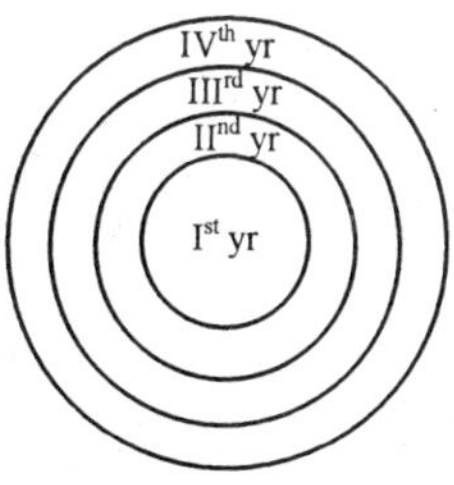

Main criticism
- Freshness of subject is lost
- Changes in teaching affect continuity of subject

(b) *Topic Method*: The whole science course is divided into a number of topics. The subjects like physics, chemistry, etc. are not treated as such, but in a correlated and integrated manner.

A topic like 'air' can include a number of lessons such as its physical properties, chemical properties, oxygen, nitrogen, respiration, ventilation, barometer and pumps.

(c) *Historical Approach*: Historical approach emphasizes the organization of the science course in accordance with the evolution of science, i.e., the stages through which science has passed in the actual course of development from the very beginning. In this approach the main emphasis is the realization of scientific life rather than the mastery of principles and methods. The pupils are directed towards the intellectual development of great man of science.

(d) *Nature's System or Nature Study*: In this system an exhaustive study of nature is aimed at. It gives training to the pupil to take interest to our surrounding, to observe natural phenomena and to draw logical conclusions from the facts observed in our daily experiences. Nature study is neither Botany or Zoology nor Physics or Chemistry. Yet it is all these and in that sense courses in nature study is broad; it establishes good relationship between child and environment.

The system does not give sound and systematic knowledge of the subject to pupil. There are number of topics in science which need theoretical analysis which is beyond the scope of nature study. Hence, it is suitable only for primary classes where people need general understanding of his environment.

Nature Sampling: In this method, the child is considered as a sampler in his environment. The material he is likely to meet with, the scientific situation he is likely to face which is chosen and are arranged in science course.

Type Study: The material to be taught is classified into types. A type is a thing or event considered as an example of class or group just as a particular plant represent a particular family of plants, a single element represent group of elements etc. These types are arranged according to the increasing order of complexity in the curriculum the pupil can make their own generalizations from the types.

General Science and Inter-disciplinary Approach: In this, an elementary study of fundamental facts and principles of various sciences are organized. It tries to explain the nature without dividing the work into biology, physics, etc. It is intended to popularize science instruction by presenting a more simple, attractive and interesting study of scientific facts and principles in relation to real things of life.

8.5. Individual Difference and Science Curricula

There are children of widely different abilities in the same class, from the different self-esteem background, different values, and different outlook. There are children who require differentiated educational programme and service beyond those normally provided by the regular school programmes. There can be enrichment programmes and remedial programmes.

Enrichment Programmes for Gifted Children

Gifted children are those by virtue of outstanding abilities are capable of high performance and are identified by professionally qualified persons.

Gifted children were considered above average in all their abilities specially in physical, social and emotional approach (Terman).

Gifted include,
Talented
Creative children → Productive thinkers
Skilled children → better performance in psychomotor abilities
Intelligent children IQ 130 or above

Enrichment Programmes

1. *Acceleration*: Skipping classes, may be in one subject, or more subjects or by some other means shortening the time spent on studies.

Special grouping: Opportunity for special education in each homogenous group based on abilities.
Enrichment: Special academic provision for various students.

Acceleration

This technique benefits the student without changing the actual educational programme. Skipping classes is the least desirable method of acceleration. Many emotional, psychological problems may arise in some children when they are not able to adjust in the new peer group. Some other methods in U.S.A. are

1. Early admission to primary school before six years.
2. Ungraded primary and middle schools.
   e.g: 6th grade child is doing 7th or 8th grade Maths or science.
3. Advanced placement.

Special grouping: grouping of students according to their abilities.

To solve the problem of gifted (as well as backward) the ability grouping should be subject-wise with differentiated criteria. For eg: in physics, there should be at least three types of courses; one for more able, other for average and for below average. I n American schools the students move from one class to another and the subject room are fixed.

Merit: In ability grouping the teaching can be modified according to the need of the students in more effective way

Demerit: Students are labeled as A & B grade.

Enrichment: is the type of activity devoted to the further development of the particular intellectual skills and talents of the gifted child.

Rich → Physical accumulation
Enrich → richness at the mental level

For the enrichment,

1. Identify and listening of gifted students in your class.
2. Identify of modifies or enrichment techniques to be given to the bright individuals.

Some qualities found in gifted;

1. reasoning;
2. abstract thinking;
3. originality;
4. curiosity;
5. creativity.

Two Types of Enrichment

1. *Horizontal, Breadth/lateral enrichment* : Enrichment can be given in relating the topic with other related topics.
   For example: while teaching photosynthesis, relation to stomato and other related metabolic activities can be taken as enrichment.
2. *Vertical depth or Intensive enrichment*: giving more intensive, detailed or indepth study of the topic.
   In India, some talent search examinations are being conducted at various levels to identify the gifted and talented.

Slow Learners/Backward Children

They are weak intellectually and emotionally-slow in learning than the average student. They are those students having IQ below average.

Educational Definition: Backward child is one who is not able to do the work of one year below. Eg: a 6th class child not able to do 5th class work. Some students may be backward in one subject not in others. The enthusiasm of slow learners tend to be short lived.

Remedial Programmes to Help Backward Children

1. Special Grouping: Identify the abilities of slow learners in an effective way, special curricula are given to them.
   Many special curricula in science have been developed in U.S.A. and U.K. – where the stress is on expectation and the materials according to the needs and characteristics. Content covered is comparatively less, more real experience are given.

2) Remedial Programme: Like enrichment programme, remedial are designed for slow learners. Programmes instruction works very well with slow learners because of self pacing.
   In Indian schools there is procession for a remedial period in the beginning or at the end of the school hour.
3) Role of the Teacher – Teacher has to be patient with slow learners, they need care and love. Teacher should help them to achieve success, encourage them to work hard.

8.6. Text Books

It is one of the important aids in the teaching learning process. It helps in giving a correct understanding of the principles and concepts of science and in developing certain skills and attitudes, in systematic and speedy revision.

Functions of Science Text-Book

1) To supplement the class work or class instruction.
2) To supplement or enrich the science syllabus.
3) For doing home work and the preparatory part of assignments.
4) For a systematic and speedy revision after the course has been finished.
5) To develop open mindedness, training in scientific method and to inculcate other scientific disciplines.
6) To help the pupil for correct understanding of basic concepts and principles of science.
7) To develop particular skillwhich may later on be of utility in life.
8) To encourage classroom discussions for arriving at accurate conclusions.

Characteristics of a good text book of Science

The Author: Certain minimum qualifications and experience for authors should be laid down by authorities.

a) The get-up (mechanical features of the text-book) (i) The quality of paper, binding, printing and type of letters used should be fine and appealing, (ii) The science book must be neatly illustrated with diagrams and sketches.

b) Subject matter (it's nature and organization):
   (i) Proper selection and organization of subject matter.
   (ii) Matter should arrange in psychological sequence.
   (iii) Book should follow aims of science education.
   (iv) Serve as a guide for demonstrations and individual experiment.
   (v) Subject matter should write in a simple clear and lucid way.
   (vi) Scientific terminology should be provided in brackets whether the books are written in regional language.
   (vii) Use only standard terminology.
   (viii) Each chapter should begin with a brief introduction and end with a summary.
   (ix) Assignment concerning application to life situation, suggestions for further reading should be included at the end of each chapter.
   (x) Provide suggestions for making improvised equipments and provision should be available for meaningful correlation.

Criteria for Selection of a Good Science Text Book

1. The level of complexity of the text corresponding to intellectual level of student.
2. The style of writing.
3. Nature of illustrations.
4. The suggested supplementary activities.
5. The provision for individual difference.
6. The clarity and organization of material.

Analysis and Evaluation of Science Text Book (Vogels Score Card)

Louis F Vogel developed an evaluation scale, that can be a guide to selecting a science text book Vogel's score card is suggestive and becomes gradually subjective. The major criteria are grouped under ten major headings:

1. Qualification of author,
2. Organization,

3. Content,
4. Presentation,
5. Accuracy,
6. Readability,
7. Adoptability,
8. Teaching aid,
9. Illustrations, and
10. Appearance.

8.7. Guide Book for Teachers

It is a ready reference material for the teacher. It contains summaries of chapters in the textbook. Conceptual development of topics, statement of instructions objectives to be realized, explanation of significant terms, facts, principles, learning experience to be provided, precautions to be taken while demonstration exercises of various kinds suited to each topic evaluation, tools, assignments for pupils. It suggests the measures to be adopted to make the instruction suitable and more effective.

Advantages

1. Equips the teacher with sufficient theoretical knowledge about what is to be taught.
2. Help to find out suitable experience.
3. Helps the teacher to adopt appropriate methods to teach every topic.
4. Helps the teacher to evaluate relevant evaluation tools after finishing even topic.

Guidelines for Preparing Science Curriculum Materials

1. Meaningful and purposeful learning experiences should be provided for students.
2. Learning styles of students should be considered when selecting and implementing innovative ideas.
3. Interesting learning experiences should be made available for student.
4. Provision should be made for diverse achievement levels of students.

5. Be in harmony with the accepted objectives set up for students.
6. Lead to the inculcation of appropriate scientific attitudes and the understanding of the methods of science.
7. Be in harmony with the needs and interest of school.
8. The course in science should be organized to provide frequent opportunity for pupil to participate in planning and to engage in individual and group projects.
9. Provision should be made for effective evaluation including self-evaluation.
10. Abundant opportunities should be given fro building principle and concepts.

9
Constructivism

Constructivism is a theory of knowledge (epistemology) that argues that humans generate knowledge and meaning from an interaction between their experiences and their ideas. During infancy, it is an interaction between their experiences and their reflexes or behaviour-patterns. Piaget called these systems of knowledge *schemata*. Constructivism is not a specific pedagogy, although it is often confused with constructionism, an educational theory developed by Seymour Papert, inspired by constructivist and experiential learning ideas of Jean Piaget. Piaget's theory of constructivist learning has had wide ranging impact on learning theories and teaching methods in education and is an underlying theme of many education reform movements.

9.1. Constructivist Learning Intervention

The Nature of the Learner

Social constructivism views each learner as a unique individual with unique needs and backgrounds. The learner is also seen as complex and multidimensional. Social constructivism not only acknowledges the uniqueness and complexity of the learner, but actually encourages, utilizes and rewards it as an integral part of the learning process (Wertsch 1997).

Importance of the Background and Culture of the Learner

Social constructivism or socioculturalism encourages the learner to arrive at his or her version of the truth, influenced by his or her background, culture or embedded worldview. Historical developments and symbol systems, such as language, logic, and mathematical systems, are inherited by the learner as a member of a particular culture and these are learned throughout the learner's life. This also stresses the importance of the nature of the learner's social interaction with knowledgeable members of the society. Without the social interaction with other more knowledgeable people, it is impossible to acquire social meaning of important symbol systems and learn how to utilize them. Young children develop their thinking abilities by interacting with other children, adults and the physical world. From the social constructivist viewpoint, it is thus important to take into account the background and culture of the learner throughout the learning process, as this background also helps to shape the knowledge and truth that the learner creates, discovers and attains in the learning process (Wertsch 1997).

The Responsibility for Learning

Furthermore, it is argued that the responsibility of learning should reside increasingly with the learner (Glasersfeld, 1989). Social constructivism thus emphasizes the importance of the learner being actively involved in the learning process, unlike previous educational viewpoints where the responsibility rested with the instructor to teach and where the learner played a passive, receptive role. Von Glasersfeld (1989) emphasized that learners construct their own understanding and that they do not simply mirror and reflect what they read. Learners look for meaning and will try to find regularity and order in the events of the world even in the absence of full or complete information.

The Harkness Discussion Method

It is called the "Harkness" discussion method because it was developed at Phillips Exeter Academy with funds donated in the 1930s by Edward Harkness. It involves students seated in a circle, motivating and controlling their own discussion. The teacher acts as little as possible. Perhaps the teacher's only function is to observe, although he/she might begin or shift or even direct a discussion. The students get it rolling, direct it, and focus it. They act as a team, cooperatively, to make it work. They all participate, but not in a competitive way. Rather, they all share in the responsibility and the goals, much as any members share in any team sport. Although the goals of any discussion will change depending upon what's under discussion, some goals will always be the same: to illuminate the subject, to unravel its mysteries, to interpret and share and learn from other points of view, to piece together the puzzle using everyone's contribution. Discussion skills are important. Everyone must be aware of how to get this discussion rolling and keep it rolling and interesting. Just as in any sport, a number of skills are necessary to work on and use at appropriate times. Everyone is expected to contribute by using these skills.

The Motivation for Learning

Another crucial assumption regarding the nature of the learner concerns the level and source of motivation for learning. According to Von Glasersfeld (1989) sustaining motivation to learn is strongly dependent on the learner's confidence in his or her potential for learning. These feelings of competence and belief in potential to solve new problems, are derived from first-hand experience of mastery of problems in the past and are much more powerful than any external acknowledgment and motivation (Prawat and Floden 1994). This links up with Vygotsky's "zone of proximal development" (Vygotsky 1978) where learners are challenged within close proximity to, yet slightly above, their current level of development. By experiencing the successful completion of challenging tasks, learners gain confidence and motivation to embark on more complex challenges.

9.2. Role of the Instructor

Instructors as Facilitators

According to the social constructivist approach, instructors have to adopt to the role of facilitators and not teachers (Bauersfeld, 1995). Whereas a teacher gives a didactic lecture that covers the subject matter, a facilitator helps the learner to get to his or her own understanding of the content. In the former scenario the learner plays a passive role and in the latter scenario the learner plays an active role in the learning process. The emphasis thus turns away from the instructor and the content, and towards the learner (Gamoran, Secada, & Marrett, 1998). This dramatic change of role implies that a facilitator needs to display a totally different set of skills than a teacher (Brownstein 2001). A teacher tells, a facilitator asks; a teacher lectures from the front, a facilitator supports from the back; a teacher gives answers according to a set curriculum, a facilitator provides guidelines and creates the environment for the learner to arrive at his or her own conclusions; a teacher mostly gives a monologue, a facilitator is in continuous dialogue with the learners (Rhodes and Bellamy, 1999). A facilitator should also be able to adapt the learning experience 'in mid-air' by taking the initiative to steer the learning experience to where the learners want to create value.

The learning environment should also be designed to support and challenge the learner's thinking (Di Vesta, 1987). While it is advocated to give the learner ownership of the problem and solution process, it is not the case that any activity or any solution is adequate. The critical goal is to support the learner in becoming an effective thinker. This can be achieved by assuming multiple roles, such as consultant and coach.

A few strategies for cooperative learning include

- Reciprocal Questioning: students work together to ask and answer questions
- Jigsaw Classroom: students become "experts" on one part of a group project and teach it to the others in their group
- Structured Controversies: Students work together to research a particular controversy (Woolfolk 2010)

Nature of the Learning Process

Social constructivism, strongly influenced by Vygotsky's (1978) work, suggests that knowledge is first constructed in a social context and is then appropriated by individuals (Bruning et al., 1999; M. Cole, 1991; Eggan & Kauchak, 2004). According to social constructivists, the process of sharing individual perspectives-called *collaborative elaboration* (Meter & Stevens, 2000)-results in learners constructing understanding together that wouldn't be possible alone (Greeno et al., 1996).

Social constructivist scholars view learning as an active process where learners should learn to discover principles, concepts and facts for themselves, hence the importance of encouraging guesswork and intuitive thinking in learners (Brown et al.1989; Ackerman 1996). In fact, for the social constructivist, reality is not something that we can discover because it does not pre-exist prior to our social invention of it. Kukla (2000) argues that reality is constructed by our own activities and that people, together as members of a society, invent the properties of the world.

Other constructivist scholars agree with this and emphasize that individuals make meanings through the interactions with each other and with the environment they live in. Knowledge is thus a product of humans and is socially and culturally constructed (Ernest 1991; Prawat and Floden 1994). McMahon (1997) agrees that learning is a social process. He further states that learning is not a process that only takes place inside our minds, nor is it a passive development of our behaviours that is shaped by external forces and that meaningful learning occurs when individuals are engaged in social activities.

Vygotsky (1978) also highlighted the convergence of the social and practical elements in learning by saying that the most significant moment in the course of intellectual development occurs when speech and practical activity, two previously completely independent lines of development, converge. Through practical activity a child constructs meaning on an intrapersonal level, while speech connects this meaning with the interpersonal world shared by the child and her/his culture.

Dynamic Interaction between Task, Instructor and Learner

A further characteristic of the role of the facilitator in the social constructivist viewpoint, is that the instructor and the learners are equally involved in learning from each other as well (Holt and Willard-Holt 2000). This means that the learning experience is both subjective and objective and requires that the instructor's culture, values and background become an essential part of the interplay between learners and tasks in the shaping of meaning. Learners compare their version of the truth with that of the instructor and fellow learners to get to a new, socially tested version of truth (Kukla 2000). The task or problem is thus the interface between the instructor and the learner (McMahon 1997). This creates a dynamic interaction between task, instructor and learner. This entails that learners and instructors should develop an awareness of each other's viewpoints and then look to their own beliefs, standards and values, thus being both subjective and objective at the same time (Savery 1994).

Some studies argue for the importance of mentoring in the process of learning (Archee and Duin 1995; Brown et al. 1989). The social constructivist model thus emphasizes the importance of the relationship between the student and the instructor in the learning process.

Some learning approaches that could harbour this interactive learning include reciprocal teaching, peer collaboration, cognitive apprenticeship, problem-based instruction, web quests, anchored instruction and other approaches that involve learning with others.

9.3. Collaboration among Learners

Learners with different skills and backgrounds should collaborate in tasks and discussions to arrive at a shared understanding of the truth in a specific field (Duffy and Jonassen, 1992).

Most social constructivist models, such as that proposed by Duffy and Jonassen (1992), also stress the need for collaboration among learners, in direct contradiction to traditional competitive approaches. One Vygotskian notion that has significant implications for peer collaboration, is that of the zone of proximal development. Defined as the distance between the actual developmental level as determined by independent problem-solving and the level of potential development as determined through problem-solving under adult guidance or in collaboration with more capable peers, it differs from the fixed biological nature of Piaget's stages of development. Through a process of 'scaffolding' a learner can be extended beyond the limitations of physical maturation to the extent that the development process lags behind the learning process (Vygotsky 1978).

Holt and Willard-Holt (2000) emphasize the concept of dynamic assessment, which is a way of assessing the true potential of learners that differs significantly from conventional tests. Here the essentially interactive nature of learning is extended to the process of assessment. Rather than viewing assessment as a process carried out by one person, such as an instructor, it is seen as a two-way process involving interaction between both instructor and learner. The role of the assessor becomes one of entering into dialogue with the persons being assessed to find out their current level of performance on any task and sharing with them possible ways in which that performance might be improved on a subsequent occasion. Thus, assessment and learning are seen as inextricably linked and not separate processes (Holt and Willard-Holt 2000).

According to this viewpoint instructors should see assessment as a continuous and interactive process that measures the achievement of the learner, the quality of the learning experience and courseware. The feedback created by the assessment process serves as a direct foundation for further development.

Selection, scope, and sequencing of the subject matter: Knowledge should not be divided into different subjects or compartments, but should be discovered as an integrated whole (McMahon 1997; Di Vesta 1987).

This also again underlines the importance of the context in which learning is presented (Brown et al. 1989). The world, in which the learner needs to operate, does not approach one in the form of different subjects, but as a complex myriad of facts, problems, dimensions, and perceptions.

Engaging and Challenging the Learner

Learners should constantly be challenged with tasks that refer to skills and knowledge just beyond their current level of mastery. This captures their motivation and builds on previous successes to enhance learner confidence (Brownstein 2001). This is in line with Vygotsky's zone of proximal development, which can be described as the distance between the actual developmental level (as determined by independent problem-solving) and the level of potential development (as determined through problem-solving under adult guidance or in collaboration with more capable peers) (Vygotsky 1978).

Vygotsky (1978) further claimed that instruction is good only when it proceeds ahead of development. It is then it awakens and rouses to life an entire set of functions in the stage of maturing, which in turn lies in the zone of proximal development. It is in this way that instruction plays an extremely important role in development.

To fully engage and challenge the learner, the task and learning environment should reflect the complexity of the environment that the learner should be able to function in at the end of learning.

Learners must not only have ownership of the learning or problem-solving process, but of the problem itself (Derry 1999).

Where the sequencing of subject matter is concerned, it is the constructivist viewpoint that the foundations of any subject may be taught to anybody at any stage in some form (Duffy and Jonassen 1992). This means that instructors should first introduce the basic ideas that give life and form to any topic or subject area, and then revisit and build upon these repeatedly. This notion has been extensively used in curricula.

It is also important for instructors to realize that although a curriculum may be set down for them, it inevitably is shaped by them into something personal that reflects their own belief systems, their thoughts and feelings about both the content of their instruction and their learners (Rhodes and Bellamy 1999). Thus, the learning experience becomes a shared enterprise. The emotions and life contexts of those involved in the learning process must therefore be considered as an integral part of learning. The goal of the learner is central in considering what is learned (Brown et al. 1989; Ackerman 1996).

The Structure of the Learning Process

It is important to achieve the right balance between the degree of structure and flexibility that is built into the learning process. Savery (1994) contends that the more structured the learning environment, the harder it is for the learners to construct meaning based on their conceptual understandings. A facilitator should structure the learning experience just enough to make sure that the students get clear guidance and parameters within which to achieve the learning objectives, yet the learning experience should be open and free enough to allow for the learners to discover, enjoy, interact and arrive at their own, socially verified version of truth.

9.4. Constructivist Approach of Generating Knowledge

Many pupils find science demanding-they find it difficult to understand relatively fundamental concepts. In the past, and possibly to a lesser extent today, subject content dominated how teachers thought about science teaching. Teaching was viewed mainly in terms of the science concepts to the exclusion of how children think and learn. To teach children successfully requires and understanding of how children think and construct scientific knowledge as well as a thorough understanding of science. Learning is an internal process that takes place within the mind. 'Constructivism', presently, is the dominant way of thinking about learning.

Learning could be viewed as simply remembering and restating what is said. This is often referred to as 'learning-by-rote' or 'drill and practise'. In this model, there is little need for a teacher to consider what is going on in the learner's minds other than perhaps to monitor whether the learning has occurred (or not). The emphasis here is placed firmly on the subject material and learning is the *transmission* of information from source to mind.

Looking at learning in this way stresses the passivity of the mind. It has become associated with studies of behaviourism and stimulus response psychology. In the past, behaviourist views of learning has been popular, however more recently in science education they have been questioned. There has been a shift in thinking about learning and teaching towards a view where learning is seen not as a passive representation but as an active reconstruction and reinterpretation of experiences. Knowledge is thought of as being actively built up or constructed by the learners as they interpret learning experience. This is constructivist view of learning.

For constructivists, learning is viewed as an interaction between the learner and the learning environment. During this interaction prior knowledge is used as a basis to interpret and construct new understanding. In effect, learning is a process in which the learner uses existing knowledge as a basis to interpret and construct new ideas. Viewed in this way, learning science concepts is a process of conceptual change and addition. And central to teaching with this agenda in mind is the understanding of how and why children 'change' their ideas. As Driver (1989) notes: "If it is accepted that learning involves the restructuring of students' conceptions then not only to educators need to appreciate the ideas that children bring to the learning situation, but they need to understand the processes by which conceptual change occurs in order that this can be taken into account in the design of learning programmes".

Driver and colleagues (1989) suggest a popular 'Constructivist' teaching sequence that offers a means of restructuring children's idea

Phase	Overview
Orientation	Teacher introduces the topic
Elicitation of ideas	Opportunities are provided for pupils to explore and explain their ideas
Restructuring of Ideas	
Clarification and exchange	Pupils are given a chance to recognize scientific ideas and examine their own ideas
Exposure to Conflict situation	Pupils are provided with situations in which to test their ideas and recognize the limitations of these ideas
Construction of new ideas	Opportunities are provided for pupils to restructure (extend, modify or replace) their ideas
Evaluation	Pupils are provided with opportunities to test out the validity of their newly constructed ideas
Application of Ideas	Pupils are provided with opportunities to apply their ideas in new situations-to reinforce these ideas
Review Change in Ideas	Pupils are provided opportunities upon how and why their ideas have changed.

A Constructivist Teaching Approach – *Driver (1989)*

In this context, the term scaffolding has been used to describe the role of teaching. As Burner (1985) writes 'the tutor in effect performs the critical function of "scaffolding" the learning task to make it possible for the children to internalize external knowledge and convert it into a tool for conscious control. 'Scaffolding' can come in a variety of forms, depending on the nature of the task. Of course, as the competence of the child increases, the teacher needs to gradually remove the support (scaffold) and the timing of this is both sensitive and crucial.

Trowbridge and Bybee (1996) present a lesson structure that takes account of recent constructivist approach and has similarities with the 'constructivist' teaching model proposed by Driver *et al.* The lesson structure is based around seven Es presented in a particular sequence. The lesson structure is shown in the following table.

Elicit:	Structure activities to find out about children's ideas about the concepts and skills you are about to explore.
Engage:	Use a series of classroom activities that engage student's interest and curiosity.
Explore:	Provide activities to explore particular phenomena and generate their own explanations of these phenomena.
Encounter:	Any misconceptions about these should be challenged. This can be achieved by setting up a series of activities that promote alternative conceptions and demonstrate the weaknesses in pupil's current understanding.
Explain:	Pupils should be provided with opportunities to explain their understanding; encourage pupils to explain concepts in their own words.
Elaborate:	This is the application phase: classroom activities should be provided for pupils to apply their new ideas in different contexts and to different situations.
Evaluate:	Pupils should be given opportunity to evaluate their own learning. They should be given a chance to explore why they have changed their ideas and the strengths of their new ideas when compared with their old ideas.

Pre-conceptions and Misconceptions of Learner

Children also have ideas and beliefs about Science. As a teacher of Science, the curriculum requires you to find out about, explore and extend children's ideas, images and beliefs Science. Like many aspects of classroom practice, when you start to scratch beneath the surface things become more complex.

To teach children successfully requires an understanding of how children think and construct scientific knowledge. Learning is viewed as an interaction between the learner and the learning environment. During this interaction prior knowledge is used as a basis to interpret and construct new understandings. In effect, learning is a process in which the learner uses existing knowledge as a basis to interpret and construct new ideas. Ausubel (1968) provides an overview of Educational Psychology, "If I had to reduce all Educational Psychology to just a single principle, I would say this: find out what the learner knows and teach him accordingly". The Science Educationist Rosalind Driver (1989) writers, "The key feature of a constructivist epistemology is that human beings construct mental models of their world and new experiences are interpreted and understood in relation to existing mental models or schema".

From the constructivist perspective, learners are seen as developing ideas through an active process in which current ideas have a fundamental role. In this light, children's ideas become highly significant as they potentially form the basis of future thinking and understanding. Hence children's misconceptions, errors or confusions result 'learning blocks'. The table below lists some common misconceptions of pupils about the nature of Science that all new teachers should be aware of.

Learner's Misconception	*Widely Accepted Viewpoint*
• Scientific theories are incontestable and true for all time.	All scientific knowledge is open to challenge and revision
• All scientific knowledge is generated by experiments and data collection	Many ideas are new and creative explanations of observed phenomena (eg: theory of evolution)
• Scientists make judgements in isolation	Many decisions involve ethical, social and economic factors (eg: whether to use animals for experiments, whether to develop weapons technology)
• Science offers solutions to problems	Not realizing that while the application of science may offer the solution to some problems it may be the cause of others.

Researchers have explored, collected and catalogued a vast array of children's alternative ideas or misconceptions in Science. In some cases confusions would seem to emanate the use of language. Some words have an everyday meaning and a particular scientific meaning can be confusing. We commonly use the word 'animal' to mean mammals other than humans, where as it has a broader meaning in Biology. We use the word 'plant' in the context of nuclear power plant 'molar' 'nucleus' and 'cell' have quite different meanings in Biology and Chemistry classes. The word 'work' has a general meaning and also a specific definition in the context of Physical Science. In other instances children's alternative ideas seem to stem from everyday informal sensory experiences. From an early age, for instance, we build up models of how objects behave when they are dropped, pushed, twisted and thrown. These ideas, needless to say, are quite different when compared with Newtonian view of the world. These ideas run contrary to scientific thinking and as a consequence can lead to further conceptual confusions.

The table below suggests some children's ideas that Science teachers should watch out for.

Concept	*Confusions*
• Osmosis	One solution diffuses into another.
• Air	Air is weightless or has negative weight.
• Matter	Matter disappears when substances dissolve or burn.
• Heat	Heat is a kind of substance, the temperature of an object depends on the kind of stuff it is made of (e.g.: metals are cold, plastics are warm); Heat and temperature same.
• Energy	Energy is primarily associated with human action/ motion; energy gets used up.
• Light	Light travels further at night than in day time.
• Particles	Macroscopic properties given to microscopic particles (particles melt, expand... etc); Space between particles not empty.
• Plant Nutrition	Plants take in food through their roots. Food for plants include anything they taken in (e.g. Water, air, sunlight, fertilizer).
• Gas exchange in man	Only CO_2 given out during expiration. Only O_2 taken in during inspiration.
• Respiration in fishes	O_2 of water molecules used for respiration.
• Diffusion	Only gaseous molecules move from higher concentration.
• Electricity	Electricity gets used up as it goes round a circuit.

It is often implied that successful constructivist teaching involves the replacement of children's ideas with more scientific ones.

Children's Science

Science is a human enterprise through which we come to some understanding of the biological and physical aspects of the world around. This understanding involves the development of ideas or concepts which enable related situations, objects or events to be linked together so that past experience enables us to make sense of new experience. Building up ideas about the scientific aspects of the world is the business of science. The ideas of science change as scientists extend their explorations and expose their theories to wider testing.

Children do not come to their science activities with empty heads, but with ideas which they have formed in earlier activities and observations, and which they use in trying to make sense of the new phenomena they encounter as their experience expands. The notion of the development as change in ideas, rather than as putting new ideas in place without consideration of anything already there, has important implications for how we go about helping this development. As children change their ideas by modifying them; so that they fit the evidence better or adopting alternative ideas.

Children tend to develop ideas which explain particular events without connecting them with ideas about other events which are in fact related. The separate ideas are brought together to form ideas which are 'bigger' in that they can be applied to a greater range of phenomena. This process continues throughout life. Once the ideas have been expressed some way, through talking, drawing, writing or indeed through action, then some useful strategies can be used for promoting change. Children can be helped to advance their ideas by putting the following strategies into operation.

- *Helping children to test out their ideas*: After finding out the child's idea, the teacher has to:
  - (i) Take the child's idea seriously.
  - (ii) Help the child turn the idea into a form to that it can be tested.
  - (iii) Help the child do it in a way which is 'fair' so that the result is really a test of the idea.
  - (iv) Help the child to interpret the results in order to establish the best explanation.

- *Using ideas and solving problems*: Without challenging children's ideas directly, children can be helped to reconsider their ideas by having to use them to solve problems. The effectiveness of the problem-solving depends on the children being motivated to solve the problem.
- *Discussion and the development of language*: While first-hand experience is essential to testing ideas, this does not deny that ideas can be acquired and modified as a result of interaction with others either in direct discussion or through reading. The act of presenting ideas to other requires putting them in some order. These experiences encourage children to reflect on and justify their ideas. In discussion they also realize that others have different ideas which may cause them to review their own or to challenge an opposing view.
- *Children representing their ideas*: Ideas can be communicated in ways other than words and the struggle to represent an idea in drawing or model can be as helpful in forcing reflection as a discussion with others. The product is useful to the teacher as an indication of the child's ideas.
- *Children's generalizations*: Attempting to make generalizations is a part of developing ideas into broader, more widely applicable ones. Children do not need much encouragement to generalize, however their tendency is to do this too readily and to be over-inclusive.

9.5. Teacher Initiated Learning vs Student Initiated Learning

Teaching initiated instruction is direct instruction that is an application of behavioural perspective of instruction. Behavioural theory of instruction establishes specific learning objectives and building a sequence of learning activities that proceed from simple to complex.

Direct instruction is often called 'whole group' or 'teacher-led' instruction. Basically, the technique involves academic focus, tends to be large group oriented and tends to emphasis factual knowledge. The following are the steps of Direct instruction:

- Review and check previous work.

- Present new material in small units.
- Provide for guided practice.
- Provide for feedback and corrections.
- Supervise independent seat work.
- Review concepts every week and every month.

The strengths of the system of teacher initiated instruction are listed below:

- Content delivered to entire class.
- Teacher controls focus of attention .
- Teacher focuses on class objectives.
- Teacher provides clarity through explanations.
- All students work on same task.
- Feedback assesses class understanding of learning.

In Student initiated instruction (Learner activated instruction) students determine how to reach the desired learning outcomes. A classroom that uses student initiated learning will be a maze of activity: small groups, working groups and individuals working on projects or activities simultaneously. There is little sequencing of instruction and the teacher can be observed moving about the room acting as prompter, question asker, clarifier- in short a facilitator of learning.

Teacher initiated instruction has an academic focus, little choice of activity for individual students, large group instruction and teacher domination over most curricular and instructional decision.

Table of Comparison

	Student Initiated Instruction	*Teacher Initiated Instruction*
1.	Flexible arranged furniture.	Somewhat fixed arrangement.
2.	Emphasis on individual or small group work.	Delivery to entire class.
3.	Teacher as facilitator.	Teacher as controller.
4.	Little concern about time.	Time used efficiently.
5.	Varied types of assessment.	Prompt delivery of feed back.
6.	Emphasis on exploration.	Emphasis on fundamentals.
7.	Flexible classroom structure.	Rigid classroom structure.
8.	Simultaneous activities.	All students on same task.
9.	Time consuming preparation.	Preparation time minimal.

9.6. Learning from Experience

In today's education system, verbalism dominates all activities. Words which are found remote or unrelated by the learner cannot initiate learning. The learners then become crammers in order to pass in the examination. To change this, learning must become rich, active, personal, interactive and adventure something. This can be achieved through providing rich experiences to the learner.

The root of the word Experience is 'experi' meaning to 'try-out'. 'Experiencing' and 'what is experienced' are not two different things. Experience cannot be limited sensation. It always comes with meaning. It has within it judgement, thought and connectivity with other experience. Experience is not simply an event which happens, it is an event with meaning. Meaning is an integral part of experience. As a meaningful encounter, it is not just an observation or a passive undergoing of something but an active engagement with the environment, of which the learner is an important part.

David Cohen and Walker (1997) have put forward the following propositions about learning from experience.

(i) Experience is the foundation of, and the stimulus for, learning.
(ii) Learners actively construct their experiences.
(iii) Learning is a holistic process of cognitive, affective and psychomotor experiences.
(iv) Learning is socially and culturally constructed.
(v) Learning is influenced by the socio-emotional context in which it occurs.

The nature of experiential learning is determined by the following factors:

(i) Learning by dong – Hence the hands on-experience, direct experience is given importance.
(ii) Personal learning through everyday experience.
(iii) Experiential social group process.
(iv) Experiential learning in the classroom with group process.

Teachers have to plan teaching strategies for learning from

experiences. Lecturing/ expository methods will have to be replaced by more interactive activity based methods. One way communication has to be replaced by two-way or multiple way communication. Use of teaching aids will have to be reduced to give way to learning aids/materials. Strategies such as Role play, Simulation exercises provide an opportunity to experience, feel and to empathize. Methods such as Laboratory work, Field trips, Discussions, Dramatization, Seminars and Projects would involve the learners as active participants in the process of learning and make their learning more challenging, enjoyable and adventurous.

10
Methods of Teaching

A teacher of science can use a variety of methods and techniques which he might use in everyday classroom teaching. The main purpose is to make interactive process effective so that meaningful learning may take place. a science teacher should use proper methods of teaching to make learning relevant and useful.

Meaning

The word 'method' in Latin means 'mode' or 'way'. In education it means the mode by which the material is communicated from the teacher to the pupil. So the method can be defined as the manner in which teachers impart knowledge and skills while teaching, and students comprehend knowledge and acquire the skills in the process of learning.

This definition clarifies that the method includes both teaching and learning.

It will be relevant to say that teaching methods have been influenced by many factors. The factors to be considered while selecting teaching methods are:

a) Educational Objectives;
b) Time and Material Factors; and
c) Teacher, Students and the Environment.

a) Educational Objectives

Methods will have to be selected with regard to the educational objectives i.e., in terms of changes to be effected in knowledge, skills and attitudes.

Each subject has its own features. In physical science, some of the topics contains principles from physics, chemistry and mathematics. The teacher should know when to use each method and how to use it.

b) Time and Material Factors

Here, material factors refers to the availability of materials, laboratory facilities, physical infrastructure, audio-visual and financial resources. Method should be selected according to the availability of materials factors.

Time is a deciding factor on the selection of method. Time required for preparation and implementation of each method is different.

c) Teacher, Students and the Environment

The knowledge, teaching experience and competence of the teacher are important factors in the selection of methods.

The learner's intellectual growth, age and interest should be taken into account while choosing a method. The social, cultural and political background of the students should also be considered. The environment plays an important role in the selection of method. For example, a method suitable for a rural background may not be applicable in an urban situation.

Grouping of Teaching Methods

There are numerous methods of teaching with common characteristics. We can categorize the methods as follows:

Oral Methods	*Activity Methods*	*Special Methods*
Narration	Demonstration method	Programmed learning
Discussion	Project method	Team teaching
Lecture method	Laboratory method	Computer Assisted Learning
Recitation	Heuristic method Discovery/Inquiry method Problem-solving method	Personalized system of instruction

Oral Methods have the following Characteristics

(i) They are teacher-centered methods
(ii) Teacher communicates information through verbal means
(iii) The learner is a passive listener.

Activity Methods have the following Common Characteristics

(i) They are learner-centered
(ii) Learning takes place due to active involvement of the learner.
(iii) The teacher functions as a facilitator of learning or as a stage setter for learning.

Special methods fulfill a specific requirement which is based on psychological theories or technological facilities. Therefore, each method has its own characteristics. However, these methods seek participation of the learner.

10.1 Lecture Method

The Lecture method is the most widely used teaching method. Research on lecturing in higher education has shown that the lecture is a robust and useful teaching method at this stage. but it has less importance for primary and secondary school stage where activity has proved much more useful.

Meaning: The lecture is an exposition of knowledge, facts, principles or other information which a teacher wishes to present to his pupils. While using this method, the teacher assumes that student possess sufficient background and ability to understand the lecture.

A science teacher should be careful in planning a lecture and should use it with the help of diagrams, charts, models and films. The teacher is only active participant and pupils are passive listners in this method. But if the lecture is properly planned, it can help in motivating, inspiring and stimulating students. One of the procedure for planning a lecture is as follows:

Aim of the lecture

↓

↓

Introduction of the topic

↓

Questions-Body of the lecture-Examples

↓

Discussion
Illustration
Demonstration

↓

Summary and Conclusion

Merits

1) It is the most economical method. A single teacher can teach a large number of pupils at a time and it is a way of getting a large amount of information across a large group.
2) Some abstract topics in science are best taught by the lecture method.
3) It simplifies the work of the teacher since much less effort is needed for preparing his lesson.

Demerits

1) Science is best learnt by doing. There is no provision for activities in this method as the students are passive listners.
2) This method does not touch the affective and psychomotor domains of the learner.
3) The rate of imparting information by the teacher may not be according to the capabilities of the learner.
4) The method is not democratic. It encourages the student to rely upon an authority.

10.2 Demonstration Method

Demonstration is a process of showing how something works or is used. It is an act to display working of some experiment. Demonstrations are concrete experiences that can be used for structuring future information for students. For example, when a chemistry teacher is showing the reaction of acid or alkali on litmus paper, he is demonstrating. When properly used, this method can be much effective and useful.

Purposes of Demonstration

Demonstration is a process of showing how something works or is used. It is an act to display working of some experiment. Demonstrations are concrete experiences that can be used for structuring future information for students. For example, when a chemistry teacher is showing the reaction of acid or alkali on litmus paper, he is demonstrating. When properly used, this method can be much effective and useful.

Purposes of Demonstration

Simpson and Anderson (1981) summarises the purpose of demonstration as follows:

1. To show method and technique e.g. Focusing a microscope.
2. To display objects or specimen e.g. Rocks, minerals, different types of flowers, part of a radio.
3. To demonstration phenomena e.g. Optical illusions, formations of a cloud in a large flask.
4. To verify facts and principles e.g. Freezing point of water is 0°C.
5. To show applications e.g. Effect of fertilizer on growth of plants.
6. To identify problems e.g. Effects of heat on metals.
7. To identify problems for e.g. Should hot or cold water be used when further investigation making ice cubes in a refrigerator?

Criteria for Good Demonstration

1. It should be planned and rehearsed well in advance.
2. The demonstration should be visible to all and the set up should be at a good height.
3. The apparatus used for demonstration should be larger in size.
4. Demonstration should be the result of active participation of the pupils and the teacher.

5. The lighting and ventilation should be adequate.
6. The apparatus should be arranged in a sequence on the table.
7. Demonstration should be in accordance with the season and available time.
8. Demonstration should be simple and speedy.

Advantages of Demonstration

1. Through demonstrations students get an opportunity to see, observe and study the real objects.
2. Since the demonstration require less equipment and material compared to individual laboratory work, it is economical.
3. The method is useful when (a) the experiment involves special skills (b) the apparatus is expensive (c) the experiment involves some danger.
4. The method is useful when quick revision is required.

Demerits

1. There is no chance to develop practical skills or the teacher alone perform the experiment.
2. In large classes many students can miss a point presented through demonstration.
3. Sometimes, lack of prior preparation or testing makes demonstration a failure.

10.3 Individual Laboratory Method

Science laboratory work is a unique way of instruction in science teaching. This method guides students to conduct experiment individually in science laboratory.

What lecture and demonstration methods are not able to give is adequately available in laboratory method. It must be a part and parcel of theory and some are left for the students to be done in the laboratory.

Organization of Laboratory Work

The science teacher should give necessary directions for the laboratory work, highlighting the precautions to be taken. The following things should be taken into account while organizing the laboratory.

1. The experiments performed by the students should not be beyond their level of comprehension, capacity and interest.
2. The students should also learn to report the results honestly.
3. Observation should be recorded.
4. The experiments, results of practical work, drawing of diagrams must be completed in the laboratory.
5. A practical file or note book should be maintained.
6. The teacher should inculcate the habit of doing analyses and making inferences by questioning the validity of data collected.
7. Apparatus should be available in proper condition and should be arranged before starting practical classes.
8. Some rules pertaining discipline in the laboratory should be displayed outside as well as inside the laboratory.
9. In some schools a group of two or three students is a common practice. The teacher should supervise whether only the brighter students are doing practicals and others are wasting their time.

Merits

1. It helps in realizing important aims and objective of teaching physical science.
2. It is a child-centered method.
3. It helps to develop the manipulative skills in students.
4. Students get a chance for learning by doing.

Demerits

1. It requires on the part of the school, a well equipped laboratory.
2. It is an expensive method.
3. Much time is wasted in conducting experiments.

10.4 Historical or Biographical Method

Historical or Biographical method is the process of establishing general facts and principles through attention to chronology and to the *evolution* or historical course of what is being studied. In this method, the topic is introduced in an anecdotal fashion when required. A skillful science teacher can motivate students by narration of the life histories, anecdotes and situations related to the subject.

Subject like chemistry, physics and astronomy have an interesting historical background and a historical treatment of these can prove very useful. The study of a particular topic can be made interesting by tracing its evolution.

While teaching Newton laws, Archemedis principle, Atomic theory etc. The teacher can resort to several interesting anecdotes.

Merits

1. The knowledge about the anecdotes related to great scientists help the students to pursue their spirit of discovery.
2. The concepts that scientific theories and principles are not absolute truths can be revealed to the pupils by this method.

Demerits

1. This method cannot be followed always, since it would result in waste of time.

10.5 Heuristic Method

If we really want to make our students scientific and rational, this method is the best method of teaching physical science. Heuristic is derived from the Greek word 'Heurisio' meaning 'I find out'. Prof. Henry E. Armstrong (1848-1937), Professor of chemistry at the Imperial College, London was a strong advocate of the heuristic method.

Heuristic method puts the pupils in the attitude of a discoverer or a researcher. He should be helped to make his own discoveries. Based on curiosity and interest, the method makes the acquisition of learning a great adventure. The urge to overcome difficulties should come within. This method was used at St. Dunstans' college of which Prof. Armstrong was a Governor.

Prof. Armstrong, in his book "The Teaching of Scientific Method" had mentioned that,

> "The infant learns by *observing and experimenting* and the growth of intelligence at this age is altogether marvellous. We have yet to learn what effect the maintenance of such an attitude, throughout the school period, will have on the individual".

Role of the Teacher

1. The teacher must act only as a guide.
2. He should be tolerant of noise, movement of students and their asking uncomfortable questions.
3. He should help the student to search for a suitable problem, keeping in mind the age, interest along with the available facilities.
4. Detailed instruction sheets should be given to the students.
5. He must create an atmosphere of freedom to encourage self development, spontaneity and self-expression.

Procedure

Each student gets a *sheet of instruction* regarding the problem assigned to him. It there is any difficulty the student can get *guidance* from the teacher. The required apparatus is supplied and the student *gathers information* from various sources. He *records his observations* and *draw inferences* from them. The teacher can ask relevant questions and thus it becomes a training in scientific method.

Merits

1. It helps to develop scientific attitude among pupils.
2. The method involves the principle of learning by doing.
3. Students develop research skills, including setting up and fitting apparatus conducting experiments and habits of neatness.

Demerits

1. It is much time consuming.
2. This method demands too much to our students. All students cannot cope with this method.
3. It is very costly because well equipped laboratory is required.
4. Competent teachers, small number of students and gifted students are requisites of this method.

10.6 Problem Method

There are many difficult and puzzling events that appear in almost all environment. Problem solving is an important approach which has its own place is science teaching.

Meaning: The planned attack on a difficulty or perplexity for the purpose of finding a satisfactory solution is called problem solving.

Aim: Aim of this method is to present the knowledge to be learnt in the form of a problem. The solution comes from activities on the part of the pupils.

Procedure: John Dewey has outlined his method in a series of steps, which have been modified and elaborated by many workers in the field. Steps of problem solving are as follows:

(i) Identifying and defining the problem.
(ii) Formulating hypotheses.
(iii) Testing hypotheses or collecting evidences on the problem.
(iv) Interpreting results.
(v) Drawing conclusions (For details, refer scientific method).

Merits

1. Children get training in problem solving in their life situation.
2. Problem solving approach is an attitude building process which helps a person to be logical and systematic.
3. The teaching-learning process become more meaningful through learning by doing.

Demerits

1. There may be shortage of equipment and material to use problem method.
2. It is a time-consuming method.
3. Competent teachers who can bring this method into practice are less in number.

10.7 The Developmental Method

This method is not as effective as problem method or heuristic method. It is useful for teaching science. Really, this method is a modified form of the problem solving method. The students in a class as a whole, solves the problem presented by teacher, with the guidance from the teacher.

Steps:

(i) *Preparation*: At this stage, after testing the previous knowledge of the students, the teacher states the aim of the lesson.

(ii) *Presentation*: The teacher presents new knowledge at this stage. Constant interaction between teacher and students, using teaching aids and other audio-visual equipment etc. are the important activities of this stage. Pupils compare or associates the new knowledge gained with the previous knowledge.

(iii) *Generalization*: The pupils are led to draw their own generalizations.

(iv) *Application*: Pupils apply the new knowledge in new situations or in life situations.

Merits

1. The constant interaction between teacher and pupils is a positive aspect of this method.

Demerits

1. This method is teacher-oriented.
2. There is no scope for developing laboratory skills.

10.8 Dalton Plan

The method was introduced by Miss. Helen Parkhurst in the Dalton High School, Massachusetts (U.S.A.) in 1920. The Dalton plan is considering the individual difference and it is against the prevailing system of classroom teaching.

Characteristics

1. Classrooms replaced by subject laboratories.
2. Children goes to these laboratories according to their convenience and work at their own speed.
3. No fixed time table.
4. The whole years work is divided into 10 parts, each for a month.
5. Assignments forms the basis of child's work.
6. Teacher acts as a supervisor.

Merits

1. The method is based on the principle of individual work, principle of freedom and principle of self-effort.
2. Instruction is individualized.
3. There is no problem of fatigue, boredom or indiscipline.

Demerits

1. There is no opportunity for developing social habits.
2. The method is very expensive.

10.9 Assignment Method

Assignment means to give a task or job to be done by students. Student need to perform certain tasks without any active participation in planning the assignment. Assignment is an integral part of learning and it involves both the teacher and students.

Role of the Teacher

1. The teacher must be able to see individual student's needs, interest and abilities so as to assign them accordingly.

2. He should divide a unit into different assignments suggested and chosen by the students.
3. He should keep a progress chart for getting an idea of individual difficulties and a time chart for submission of assignments.
4. The teacher should be able to anticipate difficulties faced by individual students and try to help them.

Merits

1. Students get raining in extra reading and extra work related to the assignment.
2. Individual differences are also give proper importance in this method.

Demerits

1. Effectiveness of the method depends on knowledge, ability and training of the teachers.
2. It requires a well equipped laboratory and good library so that students get help whenever necessary.

10.10 Supervised Study

This method is suitable in a heterogeneous class, which consists of above average, average and below average students. The problems arising from individual differences can be remedied by the supervised study.

Supervised study should promote self-learning, by adopting a practical method of teaching pupils what to study and how to study. It also brings the pupils into and intimate contact with the teacher and the process of learning.

Some of the activities suitable for supervised study are the following:

Proper practice in the reading can be given through assignments for leading. Interpretation of graph, solving scientific and mathematical problems, field trips, proper use of reference materials etc. can be given as activities. In the laboratory supervised study can be employed by diagnosing difficulty of the pupils and helping them to solve it.

Organization

(i) Extra class: Either by arranging extra class or by staying after the class and attending to the difficulties of the pupils.

(ii) Double period plan: Organization of school table in such a way that each subject has two successive periods where one can be used for theory and the other for supervised study.

(iii) Divided period plan: One period in divided into two parts-one part for theory and the other for supervised study.

(iv) Library period plan: In this period, students may work in the library on the allotted assignments by suing reference materials.

(v) A special teacher plan: A special teacher is employed to sit with the students and clarify their doubts.

Merits

1. Suitable to give individual attention to the pupils.
2. It give the pupil training in the effective use of library.
3. Develop the ability to think undependently and creativity, in the students.

Demerits

1. The method require additional or special teachers.
2. Very good library and laboratory are essential for the success of the method.

10.11 Cooperative Learning

Cooperative learning, which will be the primary focus of this workshop, is a specific kind of collaborative learning. In cooperative learning, students work together in small groups on a structured activity. They are individually accountable for their work, and the work of the group as a whole is also assessed. Cooperative groups work face-to-face and learn to work as a team.

Cooperative learning represents the most carefully structured end of the collaborative learning continuum. Defined as "the instructional use of small groups so that students work together to maximize their own and each other's learning" (Johnson et al.

1990), cooperative learning is based on the social interdependence theories of Kurt Lewin and Morton Deutsch (Deutsch, 1949; Lewin, 1935). These theories and associated research explore the influence of the structure of social interdependence on individual interaction within a given situation which, in turn, affects the outcomes of that interaction (Johnson and Johnson, 1989). Pioneers in cooperative learning, David and Roger Johnson at the University of Minnesota, Robert Slavin at Johns Hopkins University, and Elizabeth Cohen at Stanford, have devoted years of detailed research and analysis to clarify the conditions under which cooperative, competitive, or individualized goal structures affect or increase student achievement, psychological adjustment, self-esteem, and social skills.

In cooperative learning, the development of interpersonal skills is as important as the learning itself. The development of social skills in group work-learning to cooperate – is key to high quality group work. Many cooperative learning tasks are put to students with both academic objectives and social skills objectives. Many of the strategies involve assigning roles within each small group (such as recorder, participation encourager, summarizer) to ensure the positive interdependence of group participants and to enable students to practice different teamwork skills. Built into cooperative learning work is regular "group processing," a "debriefing" time where students reflect on how they are doing in order to learn how to become more effective in group learning settings (Johnson, Johnson and Holubec, 1990).

In small groups, students can share strengths and also develop their weaker skills. They develop their interpersonal skills. They learn to deal with conflict. When cooperative groups are guided by clear objectives, students engage in numerous activities that improve their understanding of subjects explored.

There is an every increasing need for interdependence in all levels of our society. Providing students with the tools to effectively work in a collaborative environment should be a priority. Cooperative Learning is one way of providing students with a well defined framework from which to learn from each other. Students work towards fulfilling academic and social skill goals that are clearly stated. It is a team approach where the success of the group depends upon everyone pulling his or her weight.

In order to create an environment in which cooperative learning can take place, three things are necessary. First, students need to feel safe, but also challenged. Second, groups need to be small enough that everyone can contribute. Third, the task students work together on must be clearly defined. The cooperative and collaborative learning techniques presented here should help make this possible for teachers.

In cooperative learning small groups provide a place where:

- learners actively participate;
- teachers become learners at times, and learners sometimes teach;
- respect is given to every member;
- projects and questions interest and challenge students;
- diversity is celebrated, and all contributions are valued;
- students learn skills for resolving conflicts when they arise;
- members draw upon their past experience and knowledge;
- goals are clearly identified and used as a guide;
- research tools such as Internet access are made available;
- students are invested in their own learning.

Students that are involved in cooperative learning achieve many social and academic benefits. Cooperative classrooms are classes where students group together to accomplish significant cooperative tasks. They are classrooms where students are likely to attain higher levels of achievement, to increase time on task, to build cross-ethnic friendships, to experience enhanced self-esteem, to build life-long interaction and communication skills, and to master the habits of mind (critical, creative and self-regulated) needed to function as productive members of society.

Initially, the teacher carefully designs meaningful tasks that require active participation of each student in the group toward a common end. At the beginning of a cooperative lesson, the teacher's role, often in cooperation with the class, is that of "task setter." As groups work on tasks, the teacher acts as a facilitator/coach moving from group to group to monitor the learning process. The teacher also provides students with on-going feedback and assessment of the group's progress.

Basic Elements

There are five basic principles fundamental to cooperative learning.

1. Face-to-Face Promotive Interaction

By using face-to-face promotive interaction, learning becomes active rather than passive. Teams encourage discussion of ideas and oral summarization. Peer assistance clarifies concepts for both helper and the student being helped. Cooperative teams help students learn to value individual differences and promote more elaborate thinking.

2. Positive Interdependence

Students must feel that they need each other in order to complete the group's task, that is, they "sink or swim together." Positive interdependence can be built into the task by jigsawing information, by limiting materials, by having a single team product, through team roles (recorder, reporter), or by randomly .y selecting one student to answer for the team. It can be built into a reward structure by assigning team points based on team averages, on members reaching a predetermined criterion, or on team improvement rather than outright grades.

3. Individual Accountability/ Personal Responsibility

Students must feel that they are each accountable for helping to complete a task and for mastering material. They must know that a "chauffeur/hitchhiker" situation will not be productive. Ways to build in individual accountability include: students take individual quizzes; each student is responsible for a specific portion of a task; each must be able to summarize another's ideas; any student may be called on at random to answer for the team.

4. Interpersonal and Collaborative Skills

These include skills for working together effectively (staying on task, summarizing, recording ideas) as well as group maintenance skills (encouraging each other). Ways to foster skill development include teacher modeling, brainstorming characteristics of "good" skills, direct practice, process observing, and reflection. Skill practice can be "tacked on" to academic lessons through games (e.g., Talking Chips) or by making social skills a separate objective to be practiced and observed.

5. Reflection/Group Processing of Interaction

Processing means giving students the time and procedures to analyze how well their groups are functioning and how well they are using the necessary collaborative skills. Processing can be individual, team-wide, or at the whole collaborative class level. Examples include: How well did I listen? Did we take turns and include everyone? How could we have coached each other better? How can the class function more smoothly?

Simple Structures

Think-Pair-Share

This is a four-step discussion strategy that incorporates wait time and aspects of cooperative learning. Students (and teachers) learn to LISTEN while a question is posed, THINK (without raising hands) of a response, PAIR with a neighbor to discuss responses, and SHARE their responses with the whole class. Time limits and transition cues help discussion move smoothly. Students are able to rehearse responses mentally and verbally, and all students have an opportunity to talk. Both students and teachers have increased opportunities to think and become involved in group discussion. (Lyman).

Three-Step Interview

This involves structured group activity with students. Using interviews/listening techniques that have been modeled, one student interviews another about an announced topic. \"en time is up, students switch roles as interviewer and interviewee. Pairs then join to form groups of four. Students take turns introducing their pair partners and sharing what the pair partners had to say. This structure can be used as a teambuilder, and also for opinion questions, predicting, evaluation, sharing book reports, etc. (Kagan)

Round Table

Roundtable can be used for brainstorming, reviewing, or practicing while also serving as a teambuilder. Sequential form: Students sit in teams of 3 or more, with one piece of paper and one pencil. The teacher asks a question which has multiple answers. Students take turns writing one answer on the paper, then passing the paper and pencil clockwise to the next person. When time is called, teams with the most correct answers are recognized. Teams reflect on their strategies and consider ways they could improve.

Numbered Heads Together

This structure is useful for quickly reviewing objective material in a fun way. The students in each team are numbered (each team might have 4 students numbered 1, 2, 3 and 4). Students coach each other on material to be mastered. Teachers pose a question and call a number. Only the students with that number are eligible to answer and earn points for their team, building both individual accountability and positive interdependence. This may be done with only one student in the class responding (sequential form), or with all the numbers, 3's for instance, responding using an Every Pupil Response technique such as cards or handsignals (simultaneous form)

Pairs Check

This is a way to structure pair work on mastery-oriented worksheets. Students work in teams of four with two sets of partners. The worksheet is set up with problems presented in pairs. The first person in each partnership does the first problem with the pair partner serving as coach, and offering exaggerated praise. After the first problem is done, partners change roles. After each pair of problems, teams of four check each others' work and, if they agree, give a team cheer or handshake. In this way students stay on task, working together toward mastery. (Kagan)

Send a Problem

Each student on a team writes a review problem on a flash card. Teams reach consensus on answers and write them on the backs of the cards. Each group's stack of questions passes to another group, which attempts to answer them and checks to see if they agree with the sending group. If not, they write their answer as an alternative. Stacks of cards can be sent to a third and fourth group. Stacks of cards are finally returned to the senders, who may discuss the alternative answers.

10.12 Collaborative Learning

Collaborative learning is a method of teaching and learning in which students team together to explore a significant question or create a meaningful project. A group of students discussing a lecture or students from different schools working together over the Internet on a shared assignment are both examples of collaborative learning.

Collaborative learning is an educational approach to teaching and learning that involves groups of learners working together to solve a problem, complete a task, or create a product. Collaborative learning is based on the idea that learning is a naturally social act in which the participants talk among themselves. It is through the talk that learning occurs.

Collaborative learning represents a significant shift away from the typical teachercentered or lecture-centered milieu in college classrooms. In collaborative classrooms, the lecturing/ listening/ note-taking process may not disappear entirely, but it lives alongside other processes that are based in students' discussion and active work with the course material. Teachers who use collaborative learning approaches tend to think of themselves less as expert transmitters of knowledge to students, and more as expert designers of intellectual experiences for students-as coaches or mid-wives of a more emergent learning process.

Collaborative learning is a situation in which two or more people learn or attempt to learn something together. Unlike individual learning, people engaged in collaborative learning capitalize on one another's resources and skills (asking one another for information, evaluating one another's ideas, monitoring one another's work, etc.).More specifically, collaborative learning is based on the model that knowledge can be created within a population where members actively interact by sharing experiences and take on asymmetry roles.

Put differently, collaborative learning refers to methodologies and environments in which learners engage in a common task where each individual depends on and is accountable to each other. These include both face-to-face conversations and computer discussions (online forums, chat rooms, etc.). Methods for examining collaborative learning processes include conversation analysis and statistical discourse analysis.

Collaborative learning is heavily rooted in Vygotsky's views that there exists an inherent social nature of learning which is shown through his theory of zone of proximal development. Often, collaborative learning is used as an umbrella term for a variety of approaches in education that involve joint intellectual effort by students or students and teachers. Thus, collaborative learning is commonly illustrated when groups of students work together to search for understanding, meaning, or solutions or to create an artifact or product of their learning. Further, collaborative learning redefines traditional student-teacher relationship in the classroom which results in controversy over whether this paradigm is more beneficial than harmful. Collaborative learning activities can include collaborative writing, group projects, joint problem solving, debates, study teams, and other activities. The approach is closely related to cooperative learning.

Collaborative learning environment in an organization enables learners to converse with contemporaries, present as well as defend ideas and perspectives, exchange diverse beliefs, question other conceptual frameworks and get actively engaged. Learning in a collaborative environment can take place at any time. It can happen when individuals are in discussion in a group or over the Internet.

Comparison of Collaborative and Cooperative Learning

Cooperative or collaborative learning is a team process where members support and rely on each other to achieve an agreed-upon goal. The classroom is an excellent place to develop team-building skills you will need later in life.

Cooperative/collaborative learning is interactive. As a team member, an individual

- develop and share a common goal.
- contribute the understanding of the problem, questions, insights and solutions.
- respond to, and work to understand, others' questions, insights and solutions. Each member empowers the other to speak and contribute, and to consider their contributions.
- are accountable to others, and they are accountable to the concerned person.
- are dependent on others, and they depend on the concerned person.

Collaborative Learning	*Cooperative Learning*
Definition:	Definition:
"Collaborative learning is based on the idea that learning is a naturally social act in which the participants talk among themselves (Gerlach, 1994). It is through the talk that learning occurs."	Cooperative learning is a successful teaching strategy in which small teams, each with students of different levels of ability, use a variety of learning activities to improve their understanding of a subject. Each member of a team is responsible not only for learning what is taught but also for helping teammates learn, thus creating an atmosphere of achievement. (U.S. Dept. of Ed. Office of Research, 1992)
Participants work together to solve a problem	Each person is responsible for a portion of the work
Many times teacher does not have a pre-set notion of the problem or solution that students will be researching	Many times the teacher already knows the problem and solution students will be working towards

11
Evaluation in Science Teaching

11.1 Concept of Evaluation

After furnishing the objectives based teaching, the teacher will apply certain evaluation techniques to ascertain the changes that has developed in the learners.

The word evaluation refers to the act or Process of determining the value of something,

Evaluation is qualitative and continuous. Construction, administration and scoring of test is called measurement. Interpreting such sores – whether they are good for a specific purpose is called evaluation. . This means that educational evaluation is possible only if the instructional objectives are determined earlier. Evaluation based on pre-determined objectives is called objective-based evaluation.

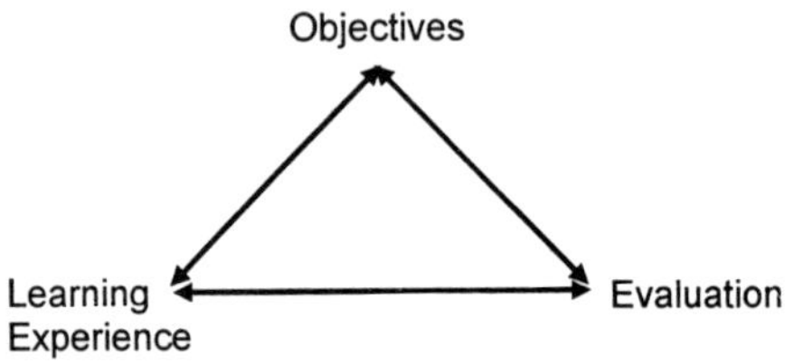

Functions of Evaluation

1. *Evaluation enhances the quality of teaching*: Through evaluation, teachers are able to find out how far they have been successful in achieving the objectives of education they had in mind. In other words they are able to assess

the degree to which they have succeeded in their teaching. This assessment leading to value judgment enables them to adopt appropriate instructional strategies and thus ensure realization of the anticipated educational objectives.

2. *Evaluation helps in clarifying the objectives*: Evaluation is based on objectives. Through this objective based evaluation the teacher gets a deeper insight into the various aspects of the topics to be taught. In the objective based approach each learning aspect has to be translated into operational behavioural terms. This analysis makes the objectives also transparent.
3. *Evaluation motivates learners*: The students try to learn the topics well because they know that their learning will be continuously evaluated. The tests used for evaluation are constructed on the basis of the syllabus in that subject. Hence, a student tries to learn the subject thoroughly so that he can succeed at the various stages of evaluation.
4. *Guidance can be given on the basis of evaluation*: Evaluation makes the individual differences clear. Specific difficulties are identified and diagnosed. Hence, it is of great utility in giving educational guidance. On the basis of the measurement of abilities also the child can be given educational and vocational guidance.
5. *Evaluation can help in bringing changes in the curriculum*: The world is progressing at quite a rapid pace these days. The new investigations in the field of education are presenting new principles and strategies before us. These are indicative of the fact that the curriculum cannot remain static. It should always go on changing. Educational evaluation provides us the direction for bringing about such changes.

11.2. Types of Evaluation-Formative and Summative

1. *Formative Evaluation*: While teaching, the content to be taught is presented in the form of small teaching points with a view to facilitate easy assimilation. At the end of each of such item, students have to be evaluated with respect to the anticipated objectives. Thus, weaknesses, if

any, should be diagnosed and remediated. This procedure will ensure mastery of the subject in terms of realization of educational objectives. As this function of evaluation is developmental in nature, it may be said to be formative evaluation. Formative evaluation provides immediate feedback leading to diagnosis and remediation and the resulting reinforcement and motivation. The instructional process thus becomes dynamic and effective through continuous formative evaluation. The emphasis is on the realization of pre-determined objectives.

2. *Summative Evaluation*: As the term indicates, summative evaluation is done at the end of something attempted. It may be conducted at the end of a unit, after it is successfully completed as evidenced by formative evaluation. Or, it may be at the end of a term and cover a number of learning units. Annual examination also may be said to summative in nature. The result of summative evaluation will give a general picture of the level of attainment, again in terms of broader instructional objectives anticipated. This also will help to reinforce teachers and pupils alike and will make instruction more effective. In addition to these functions it may aim at placement, prediction, etc. of the learners, as in the case of an annual examination or a competitive test.

The present system of instruction is based on pre-determined objectives. The teacher has to assess how far the objectives have been achieved. In order to assess the degree of realization of the objectives by the learner, the teacher has to conduct a test which is known as an achievement test. Why a particular learner could not achieve the objectives, can also be determined in terms of gaps, difficulties, etc. A test meant for that purpose is diagnostic test. The future prospects of success of a student in any selected area can be predicted by giving a test designed for the purpose. Such a test is known as a prognostic test.

11.3. Achievement Test

Every teacher wants to find out the progress made by his pupil in the subject he teaches. Achievement in a subject at a particular stage has to be assessed in terms of his mastery in the curricular provisions anticipated for that stage as well as the realization of the objectives expected. A test designed to assess the achievement in any subject with regard to set of predetermined objectives is called an achievement test.

1. *Characteristics of an Achievement Test*

(i) It measures how much a student has achieved.
(ii) It gives due weightage to objectives, content, forms of questions and difficulty levels in general way.
(iii) It gives proportional weightage to every topic in the content area in broad manner.
(iv) It strictly observes the time factor, that is, achievement is assessed through the performance of the student within a span of time allotted. No extra time is allowed.
(v) Marks scored are crucial in achievement tests. This is because, it aims at placement of pupils according to ranks.

2. *Functions of an Achievement Test*

(i) To see how effectively the teaching and learning have taken place
(ii) To motivate students before a new assignment is taken up.
(iii) To provide basis for promotion to the next stage.
(iv) To help in determining the placement of students in a particular section.

11.4. Construction of an Achievement Test

Since evaluation is an integral part of teaching and learning, students are observed in various situations continuously with a view to assess their level of achievement in terms of what has been expected of them. For this, classroom tests are frequently administered. These may be administered after completion of every unit of teaching. This enables the teacher to know the rate of progress of students as well as the extent of attainment of objectives of learning the unit. Various steps are involved in the construction of such an achievement test.

Steps involved in the construction of an achievement test

The major steps involved in the construction of an achievement test include:

1. Planning of the test;
2. Preparation of a design;
3. Preparation of the Blue print;
4. Writing of items;
5. Preparation of the scoring key and marking scheme, and
6. Preparation of question wise analysis.

1. *Planning of an Achievement Test*: A test is meant to serve many essential and important purposes. Therefore, it should be well-planned and systematically developed. Before constructing a good achievement test, the paper setter should think about the following aspects as part of his planning.
   The first consideration which is of utmost importance is what the paper setter intends to find out through the achievement test. There are certain outcomes of learning which any teacher would like to realize by teaching every unit. The paper setter should aim at testing the achievement of these objectives.
   The next step is to determine the maximum time, maximum marks and the nature of the test. These should be decided in terms of the nature and scope of the sub units or units involved in the testing.
2. *Preparation of a Design for the Test*: After determining the broad scope of the test, a design has to be developed in tune with it. The objectives, content, forms of questions, the difficulty levels of items, scheme of options, and scheme of sections are the most important factors to be considered in such a design.
   (i) *Weightage to Objectives*: This indicates what objectives are to be tested and what weightage has to be given to each objective. Suppose the teacher wants to make his pupils acquire knowledge of certain facts, develop understandings of certain concepts and principles, the ability to apply these in new situations and the skill to perform certain tasks, while teaching the specific

subject matter for which the test is being designed. Then he might include these four objectives in the design for the achievement test. He should decide the relative importance of each these objectives after carefully studying the prescribed curriculum and in tune with the nature of the content covered. This step will ensure objective-based-ness to the test, which is required scientific evaluation.

(ii) *Weightage to Content*: This indicates the various aspects of the content to be tested and the weightage to be given to each of these aspects. Suppose a lesson or unit including various aspects of study or subunits has been taught. To test these aspects/ subunits, questions covering all the aspects/ subunits should be included in the design with due weightage assigned to each aspect/subunit in relation to its importance with the other aspects. If the test is covering a number of units taught over a term for the whole year appropriate weightage is to be given to all the units.

(iii) *Weightage Type of Questions*: This indicates the forms of the questions (objective type, short answer type, and essay type) to be included in the test and the weightage to each form of questions. The setter should select those types of questions that are suitable to the objectives and content to be tested. If we ask only essay type questions we cannot get a satisfactory content coverage. This defect can be rectified by including short answer type and objective type questions also. These type of questions will add to the objectivity of the test, which is a quality warranted by a good measuring tool. The weightage to be given to each form of question should be decided on the basis of the time needed for answering, difficulty level, objectives tested and the nature of the content involved.

(iv) *Weightage to Difficulty Level*: Propriety should be shown with regard to the difficulty level of the questions asked. The test should cater to the bright, the average, and the dull. Discriminating power that is the ability to discriminate high-achievers, average achievers, and low-achievers is a quality to be maintained by a good test. If all the items are either too difficulty or too easy the test cannot discriminate the levels of achievement. Hence the test should contain easy, and difficult questions.

(v) *Scheme of Option*: Scheme of option means the option or choices given to the students to select certain questions. There may be external option as well as internal option. External option (over-all option) means the choice is given to the students for selecting a given number of questions only from among the total number of questions provided. For example, the students are asked to attempt any eight questions out of the given ten. But in case of internal option, the choice is given within a question. For example, write an essay on one of the following, write short notes on any two of the following, etc. If choice is given, the questions given for choice should be comparable in all respects.

(vi) *Scheme of Sections*: Scheme of sections means the arrangement of questions into separate divisions. For example, the question paper carrying objective type, short answer type and essay type questions can be divided into Section A, Section B and Section C.

3. *Preparation of a Blue Print*: A blue print gives the details of the design in concrete terms. Blue print is prepared as a three dimensional chart indicating the distribution of questions objective-wise, content-wise and form-wise. Some people make it four dimensional adding difficulty level also as one of the dimensions. The blue print gives the frame work for the test and indicates the broad limit within which the test constructor has to work.
4. *Writing of Items*: The blue print gives a very clear idea about the number of questions to be written from each topic, their forms and objectives. With this precise directive suggested by the blue-print, the paper setter can start writing items according to the requirements. The difficulty level also has to be considered while writing items. It should also be checked whether all the questions included can be answered within the time allotted. Construction of

test items calls for the mastery of the subject matter and technique of constructing each type of test item. If a pool of well prepared items in the form of a Question Bank is available, the constructor can easily choose the required number of items for the test in tune with the specifications of the blue print.

After writing the preliminary details such as the name of the examination, title of the paper, maximum marks and time, instruction for answering each part, etc. the setter has to arrange the questions already written. It is advisable to arrange questions in the order of their difficulty level. Normally, knowledge-item will be easier than an understanding item, which in turn may be easier than an application item. This need not be always true, but may be taken as a clue for arranging questions in a test. Items for each section can then be arranged.

5. *Preparation of the Scoring Key and the Marking Scheme*: In order to maintain objectivity, scoring should be made strictly in accordance with a pre-designed scheme of evaluation. So it is essential to prepare the scoring key and the marking scheme simultaneously with the question paper. In the case of objective type items where the answers are in the form of some letter or other symbol, a scoring key is prepared. Normally no partial credit is given for an objective type item. In the case of short answer and essay type questions, the *marking scheme* is prepared. In preparing marking scheme what the examiner has to do is to list out the value points to be credited and then to fix up the mark to be given to each value point. Clearly writing the value points will also help to identify defects, if any, that might have accidentally crept into the test items and these could be corrected before the final test is released.

   Usually, general instructions also are given at the end of the scheme of valuation in order to avoid subjectivity in scoring. Here indication may be given as to the penalty for committing errors, spelling mistakes, grammatical mistakes, etc.
6. *Preparation of Question-wise Analysis*: In order to avoid all loopholes, the setter prepares a table containing all relevant details of all the items of the test. This is done by

making an analysis of each item in terms of content material objective, specification, form of question, difficulty level, marks and estimated time. This analysis is very helpful to check whether all the aspects envisaged in the design and blue-print are satisfied by the test in its final form. If some mistake is noticed it should be rectified at this final stage.

11.5. Qualities of a Good Test

1. *Objective baseness*: The test should be based on pre-determined objectives. The setter should have definite idea about the objective behind each item. Also the objectives taken together should be in accordance with the weightage given in the design.
2. *Objectivity*: A test is said to be objective if it is free from personal biases in scoring. Objectivity is the opposite of subjectivity. A test becomes subjective when the questions are vague or loosely stated and the scoring depends upon the arbitrary judgements of examiners. Objectivity of a test can be increased by using more objective type test items and the answers are scored according to model answers provided. Objectivity is the most primary pre-requisite required for maintaining all other qualities of a good test.
3. *Validity*: A test is said to be valid if it measures what it intends to measure. When critically examined from this point of view, most of the teacher made tests are not valid. A test meant for measuring scientific knowledge should only measure scientific knowledge and not linguistic ability. Suppose a teacher of English while teaching a lesson dictates the answer of a question based upon the content of the lesson. In the examination the teacher asks the same question with the objective 'students write ideas in English Language correctly and systematically'. A student who has not developed this ability at all can score very high marks by memorizing the given answer and reproducing it mechanically even without properly understanding the meaning. Then, what is measured here is not what was really intended to measure. Hence the test is not valid. In science, suppose, in order to test the

ability to apply a principle an item the answer for which has already been given is asked. If the student has minimized the answer in advance, he can score full marks, but this need not show the ability to apply. Hence it is not valid.

It is not sufficient that what is measured includes what has been intended to measure. The test should measure all that is required to be measured. Also it should not measure anything that is unwanted. Validity thus depends upon a number of factors and hence different types of validities become significant. A test will have operational validity if the tasks required by the test are sufficient to evaluate and measure the defined activities or qualities. Predictive validity is the extent to which a test is efficient in predicting or forecasting a particular behaviour. If the items in the test constitute a representative sample of the total course content to be tested, the test can be said to have content validity. When the traits to be measured are not directly observable, what the examiner has to do is to operationally define the traits by associating them with certain observable behaviours that might project the trait. In other words, the trait is associated with something constructed by the tester to represent the traits, that is a 'construct'. Such a test is critically examined by asking the question how well the test score corresponds to the construct and hence such validity is known as construct validity. Validity of a test is often determined by correlating the scores that test with the scores obtained by the same group on some other tool of the same content, say another standardized test of known validity. This is usually named as congruent validity. Of these, the content validity and congruent validity are specially significant in standardizing an achievement test.

4. *Reliability*: Reliability of a test refers to the degree of consistency with which it measures what it is intended to measure. For example, think of a test in English Language administered to a class of forty students on the basis of which they were ranked in terms of their language achievement. Suppose without giving opportunity to improve their linguistic attainment the same test is given

to the same group after a period of one week. If the result of the test is reliable the ranking of the students in the two tests should not be very different. On the other hand, if the first rank holder in the first list becomes the fifteenth rank holder in the second and the twentieth rank holder in the first instance secures the third rank later, we cannot rely on the result and pass judgement about the exact nature of their linguistic attainment. In technical language, the test does not exhibit consistency in the results and hence it is not a reliable tool. This is true in the case of science also.

If a test is not reliable it cannot be valid because if we are getting different results on different administrations of the same test to the same group, it is evident that we are not measuring what exactly is to be measured. A test may be reliable but need not be valid. This is because it may yield consistent scores, but these scores need not represent what exactly we want to measure. A test with a high validity will normally be reliable also. This is because, if we are measuring what we really want to measure there is not much scope for inconsistency.

There are different methods for determining the reliability of a test. In the test-retest method, a test is administered twice to the same group with a short interval. The scores are tabulated and the correlation calculated. The higher the correlation, the more the reliability. In split half method, the scores of odd and even items are taken and the correlation between the two sets of scores determined. The assumption is that these scores are comparable. A high correlation suggests high reliability. In parallel form method, reliability is determined using two equivalent forms of the same test content. Here two such tests are prepared and administered to the same group one after the other. These test forms should be identical with respect to the number of items, content, difficulty level, etc. Here also comparison is made by determining the correlation between the two sets of scores obtained by the group in the two tests.

5. *Discriminating Power*: A test should be able to discriminate

the respondents on the basis of the phenomena measured. For example, an achievement test has the function of grading the examinees and ranking them. Suppose all the questions in a test are too simple for the standard of the student. All students may score high and hence discrimination which is often required for proper evaluation becomes impossible. In the same way, if all the items in a test are too difficult for the students, the majority cannot answer and hence discrimination will be difficult. The discriminating power may be considered at two levels- for the whole test and for each item of the test. The former can be maintained by preparing a design showing the percentage of items belonging to different levels of difficulty and constructing items accordingly. This will enable students with higher achievement levels secure higher scores than their counter-parts whose achievement is at a lower level. This in turn, will help in grading them accordingly. The discriminating power of an item will be evident if it is answered correctly by more high-achievers than low-achievers. When standardizing tests, the discriminating power of every item included is determined in advance and suitability from that point of view established.

6. *Practicability*: A test, even if it satisfies all the above criteria, may be useless unless it is not feasible. For example, suppose in order to ensure comprehensiveness, it was felt that thousand items should be given to be answered in ten hours. This may yield valid results, but from the practical point of view, it may not be possible to conduct such a test. Economy of time, effort, number of personnel and finance required also has to be of utmost concern for the planner of a test.
7. *Comparability*: A test possesses comparability when scores obtained by administering can be interpreted in terms of a common base that has a natural or accepted meaning. There are two methods for establishing the comparability of standard tests. They are making available equivalent forms of a test and making available adequate norms.
8. *Utility*: Utility of a test may be considered as the final

master criterion. A test has utility if it provides the test conditions that would facilitate realization of the purpose for which it is meant. For achieving utility it is essential that the test is constructed in the light of well-thought out purpose and its interpretations are used in obtaining desirable results.

9. *Comprehensiveness*: The tests should cover the whole syllabus. Due importance should also be given to each topic. The test should cover the whole areas of behaviour.

11.6. Diagnostic Test

Since learners' progress is to be appraised in terms of desirable educational objectives, it is necessary to identify deficiencies in the level of achievement together with the reasons for these deficiencies. If these are not rectified then and there they might accumulate and after a stage; learning might become quite impossible. It is here that the teacher is required to know the specific weakness of these pupils both individually and collectively and provide suitable remedial teaching. To locate the specific weakness in the learning of his pupils, the teacher can construct a test, meant for this purpose which is known as a diagnostic test. It measures how much a student has not been able to achieve in the normal teaching-learning process and why.

Remediation: Once a diagnostic test is administered and the scripts are scores the most important stage of the whole process comes up, that is the interpretation of the results of the test. For doing this, the answers of the pupils should be analyzed minutely and the deficiencies regarding each student recorded. The difficulties found common to a significantly large number of the pupils should be isolated for suitable remediation programme for the group. The remediation is nothing but the re-teaching giving fresh learning experiences meant for the removal of difficulties. It would be better to administer a parallel diagnostic test, after the remediation programme to ascertain the effectiveness of the remediation. Individual difficulties also have to be remedial but not in the group as a whole.

Prognostic Test

The test which predict the future performance of a student in the particular area is known as a prognostic test. This would help to avoid wastage that is like to occur when a student who is sure to be a misfit in a particular course of study gets admitted to that course. For example, if a student who takes a prognostic test meant to predict his expected performance in higher studies in science fairs poorly, there is no justification in admitting him for that course. Related aptitudes, interests insights, etc. can be used in the development of a prognostic test.

12
Co-curricular Activities

12.1. Science Laboratories

Introduction

The modern trend in the teaching of science is to emphasize student investigative activity as an integral part of the instructional process. Many programmes have been developed in an attempt to integrate inquiry with science instruction and to develop student inquiry skills. The scientific revolution which has been going on in all parts of the world throws light to the need of overhauling the instructional procedure of the present day. This has necessitated thinking both in the construction of science laboratories and conducting of laboratory work. The UNESCO planning mission report on science teaching, emphasized the importance of laboratory work in science teaching. They recommended the establishment of study room's in place of conventional science laboratories. Through these study rooms it is possible for the science laboratories. Through these study rooms it is possible for the science teachers to realize the following process objectives of science teaching.

(a) Illustration of abstract scientific understandings.
(b) Development of scientific concepts and principles.
(c) Development of scientific skill, attitude, interest and appreciation.
(d) An educational device for providing training in scientific method and
(e) The awakening and maintenance of curiosity in the environment.

Design of Science Laboratory for High School

In 1964 experts from the UNESCO at the invitation of the Ministry of Education, Government of India studied the stages of school science teaching in all its varied aspects. In regard to science laboratories some important recommendations were made.

They suggested the establishment of study rooms (63 sq. metres for 36 studnets) which may be used for varied types of activities' by the pupils such as writing, listening, drawing sketches, and carrying out practical work. It should provide all possible facilities for stimulating and developing out of class activities, there by scientific attitudes and abilities of the pupils can be developed. There should be a demonstration table (2500 × 300 × 580 mm) situated on a platform of 200 mm high with a view to make demonstrations clearly visible to students. There should be a blackboard (4040 × 280 mm). A stand for maps and diagrams and other teaching aids. There should be facilities for electricity. AC and DC, water and gas supply storage batteries, reservoir of water and other suitable heating devices may be used in the absence of the above facilities. For Biology, besides the study room, there should be a provision for zoo corner in the school premises as ours is a tropical country. Cages for birds and animals, terrarium and aquaria and a suitable plot of land in the shade are necessary for making scientific observation and experiments.

For performing experiments by pupils the commission recommended working table of 1250 × 845 mm where two students can share a table. The tables are fitted with electrical power points. Water supply taps, gas burner and sink. There should be a room for laboratory assistant, (total area 48 sq metres) which can also be used as a store. It is also a place where the teacher can take trial in setting up experiments for demonstrations. It should contain two tables, a writing table for the teacher and another one for the laboratory assistant, supplied with water and gas. The study rooms should be a nice place to work inside. Suitable colour combinations may be used in study rooms. The strain on the eyes of the pupils may be reduced. The colours suggested are dark green biology study room table tops, light green (under structure of tables and plank in the middle of walls) brown and light brown (table tops in physics and chemistry study roots) cream or deep cream (planks in the middle of the walls) and white ceiling and the upper part of the walls.

Selection and Purchase of Apparatus

The science teacher should prepare a list of experiments to be performed by the pupils and demonstrated by the teacher. The list of apparatus and materials to be purchased must be prepared according to the details of the above experiments. In general, for experiments to be done by the pupils as many sets of apparatus as the number working at a time and for demonstration of experiments one set for each may be purchased. It would be better to buy a few additional articles to guard against breakage.

When a number of items have to be deleted from the list in order to balance the budget, the most costly and least used apparatus may be eliminated. It is always better to divide the list into two sections the essentials and the desires. Only articles which are really to be used should be purchased. When the most urgent requirements for the practical work have been fulfilled and enough apparatus secured for demonstration the teacher should think purchasing costly articles such as projector camera, moulds of scientific appliances like steam engine, telephone model, etc. The teacher must also give due consideration to all the different parts of a subject in preparing the list. In the list full specification of articles should be given for example. The quality, the capacity, the make of flasks, retorts etc. The size of the glass jars, troughs etc. may also be mentioned. After finalizing the list of apparatus the teacher can invite quotations from three or four leading science firms. It is wise to select a reliable firm which has a fine reputation. If possible the teacher must select the apparatus himself and get them packed in his presence so as to avoid the trouble of sending back unsuitable materials. The case should be carefully unpacked and after checking with the list of articles they should be entered in the stock register and arranged in the almirahs.

Laboratory Management

All the apparatus should be arranged subject wise in different almirhas. The glass apparatus must be kept in separate shelf. The chemicals shall be arranged in alphabet order with the letter of the alphabet fixed on the self. There shall be two open shelves fixed on the walls on either side of the recesses for balance for placing the acids and regent bottles. In one shelf should be placed glass stopper bottles containing solutions, of ammonia soidum hydroxide NaOH, $AgNO_3$, $FeSO_4$, $BaNO_3$, $BaCl_2$, $CuSO_4$, litmus, etc. There may be another shelf for keeping common acids. Both dilute and concentrated chemicals such as NaCl, Na_2CO_3, MnO_2, $NaClO_3$, etc. may be kept in bottles. The bottles should be provided with labels, neatly typed.

The apparatus kept in the almirahs should be regularly inspected tested cleaned and occasionally polished. If needed Vaseline should be applied on screws and hinges of iron parts to prevent rusting. The laboratory should present an artistic appearance. This is possible only when everything is arranged systematically in the places and are replaced immediately after use.

Apparatus when not in use should not be allowed to remain outside. Neatness orderliness and cleanliness must be the motto of science teaching. The walls of the laboratory must be decorated with the pictures of scientists and diagrams of apparatus and chemical processes. An expert attender under the direction of the science teacher will attend to the keep up of the laboratory and arrangement for practical work. A laboratory workshop is also desirable to repair simple defects of the apparatus.

Laboratory Discipline

Laboratory is a place of potential dangers. Hence the science teacher must be the supreme authority in the laboratory and he should see that his orders are strictly observed by the pupils. The sign of good discipline is an atmosphere of healthy work. The following are some suggestions for the maintenance of discipline in the laboratory.

1. No pupil's should be allowed to enter the laboratory in the absence, of the teacher.
2. Every student should have a place assigned to him where he will perform his experiment.
3. Reagent bottles should be returned to the shelf immediately after use and should not be misplaced.
4. Waste filter papers, burnt up match sticks etc. should not be thrown into sinks. Waste boxes should be kept for his purpose.
5. Drawing figures on furniture should never be permitted.
6. All unnecessary talks should be avoid and playing with the apparatus should be prohibited.

7. The work should be finished five minutes before the end of the period. The apparatus should be disconnected washed if necessary and replaced in their proper places.
8. Any breakage of apparatus should be noted down in the breakage register.
9. Any deliberate destruction to scientific articles or furniture should be severely dealt with.
10. A scientific atmosphere should be kept up.
11. Those who finish their work should go to the writing table finish their record work.
12. The work done with discipline and care will be more effective and beneficial to students.

Incidents in the Laboratory

Accidents are common the laboratory. Hence the science teacher has a legal as well as moral responsibility to see that the pupils are as far as possible free from the dangers of the laboratory. The teacher should warm the pupils about the specific danger of various equipments. He should see that pupils know thoroughly well how to do the particular experiments before they actually do them. Dangerous chemicals should not be kept in open shelves. The substance must be property labelled and the pupils must pick up the practice of looking twice before using the content of the bottles. Indiscriminate experimentation should be strictly prevented. Proper maintaining of discipline will be very helpful in preventing accidents. The experiment should not be started without the permission of the teacher science accidents very often occur in the setting up of the apparatus.

Some substances which are to be handled with care are the following:

1. Concentric acids
2. Strong alkalies
3. Gases such as H_2S, SO_2, Cl_2 and CO
4. Inflammable substances like petrol, alcohol CS_2 etc.
5. Salts of Pb, Hg, Zn.
6. Explosive substances like chlorides.

First Aid

Accidents usually occur in the laboratory. It is essential that a first aid kit should be kept in every laboratory in a separate cupboard. It must contain bandages, cotton plaster tincture iodine, boric acid, sodium bicarbonate, carbolic acid, Dettol Vaseline etc. A list of the contents should be pasted on the inside of the cupboard in order to facilitate checking. A list of common accidents and their remedies approved by a good doctor should be hung up near the cupboard.

Some Common Cases of First Aid Treatment

1. *Cuts and Wounds:* To be treated with tincture iodine on cotton – no washing unless the wound is dirty.
2. *Dry burns:* Prevent contact with air either by covering it with line soaked in Vaseline or olive oil.
3. *Acid burns:*Must be washed immediately with large quantities of water and then with $NaHCO_3$ solution.
4. *Alkali burns:* Wash with running water and then with weak acetic acid or lemon juice.
5. *Phosphorous burns:* Wash with water and cover with cotton wool soaked in $AgNO_3$ solution.
6. *Eye injuries:* Should be dealt with by the doctor. The following preliminary treatment is essential in some cases.
   (i) *Acid in the eye*: The eye should be opened and closed under water. It should be washed with 1% solution of sodium bicarbonate.
   (ii) *Alkali in the eye*: The eye should be thoroughly washed with water and then with a solution of 1% boric acid.

In the case of poisons medical advice should be immediately sought. The general treatment is to remove poison by washing and by using purgatives or emetics followed by demulcents. Emetics should not be used with corrosives such as acids and alkalies. The common emetics used as sodium chloride and mustard oil. The demulcents are white of egg, milk olive oil etc. In the case of gas poisoning the patient must at once be taken into the fresh air and his clothes must be loosened. Artificial respiration must be given if necessary.

If a person's clothes catch fire he should be wrapped tightly in a fire proof blanket. If some inflammable substance gets ignited in a beaker or flask, the first can be extinguished and prevented from spreading by pressing a sheet of asbestos over the mouth of the vessel. Small fires due to oil phosphorous, sodium etc. can be put out by smothering them with large quantity of dry sand. If the first its due to gas or electricity the source of supply or the main connection should be cut off.

Physical Science Lab Safety Rules for Students

1. Always obtain your teacher's permission before beginning an activity. Listen for any special instructions the teacher gives you before the lab begins.
2. Study the procedure. If you have questions, ask your teacher. Be sure you understand any safety symbols shown on your lab page.
3. Use the safety equipment provided for you. Know the location and proper use of the fire extinguisher, eyewash station, fire blanket, and fire alarm.
4. Horseplay is intolerable and will result in immediate removal from the lab.
5. Never eat or drink in the lab, and never use glassware as food or drink containers. Never inhale chemicals. Do not taste any substances.
6. If you spill any chemical, wash it off immediately with water. Report the spill immediately to your teacher.
7. Keep all materials away from open flames. Tie back long hair and do not wear loose clothing. Wear closed-toed shoes.
8. If a fire should break out in the classroom, or if your clothing should catch fire, smother it with the fire blanket. Never Run.
9. Report any accident or injury, no matter how small, to your teacher.
10. When you are cleaning up...
    (i) Turn off the water. Disconnect electrical devices.
    (ii) Dispose of all chemicals according to the teacher's directions.
    (iii) Return all materials to their proper places.
    (iv) Place broken glass and solid substances in the proper containers.
    (v) Never discard materials in the sink.
    (vi) Clean your work area.
    (vii) Wash your hands thoroughly after working in the laboratory.

12.2. Improvised Articles or Home made Apparatus

The improvising or making of useful apparatus from common articles found in the environment has immense educational value. The apparatus devised and made in the school laboratory or workshop by the teacher or the pupils is called home made apparatus. If the teacher is resourceful and enthusiastic he can secure the help of those pupils who have an aptitude for mechanical work. These pupils will not only get a training in elementary workshop practice, but also an added interest in the subject preparation of homemade apparatus may be planned as a series of projects which would be of much educative value. The science teacher should also get the close co-operation of the craft teacher in the making of different types of apparatus. A teacher with imagination and skill will be able to make several useful appliances out of the common materials such as tins, screws, nails, corks, packing cases, etc. Some of the apparatus that can be made easily in the laboratory are test tube stands and test tube holders, inclined plane, pulleys models of pumps, Newton's disc, pinhole camera, voltaic cell, electro magnets etc.

Advantages

1. It is economic
2. It helps the teacher to introduce variety in to the nature of experiments.
3. The pupils are encouraged to devise and prepare apparatus as a hobby.
4. The application of science to everyday life is made more evident.
5. It helps in securing motivation and developing interest.
6. Science is correlated motivation and developing interest.
7. It provides training to pupils' resourcefulness and manual skill.
8. The pupils are enabled to appreciate the takes and difficulties of great scientists.

12.3. Science Club

Science club forms the back bone of the school sponsored co-curricular activities in science. They are useful agencies for spreading scientific knowledge and initiating important research work among the students. An organization which caters for the inculcation of scientific attitude, genuine interest in science and scientific activities which supplement the work of the classroom and give the content of the syllabus a practical bias may be called a science club.

Though the science club the learning of science becomes joyful and pupils learn things without the conscious effort on their part and pursue it as a pleasant hobby.

Science club movement in India is of recent origin. It began in 1957-58 under the auspices of the DEPSE which assisted financially to the tune of Rs. 1200/- per science club in the country. According to an NCERT publication there were about, 900 science clubs in the country in the year 1974. The success of the science club depends on the factors such as the Science Teacher Accommodation, material, proper guidance, motivation and follow-up programmes.

Aims of Science Club

1. To encourage the pursuit of Science as a hobby.
2. To develop a general interest in Science.
3. To inculcate scientific attitude and providing training in scientific method.
4. To encourage individual and group activities.
5. To understand the importance of science in everyday life.
6. To stimulate the active participation and initiative of pupils in learning science.
7. To develop in children healthy competition.
8. To keep the students in touch with the recent advances in science.
9. To exchange information and activities with other clubs.

Organization

The science teacher, in an informal talk with the class can explain the importance and benefits of science club and thus arouse the enthusiasm of the pupils. The discussion is followed by a business meeting in which the various office bearers are chosen. Every science club must have a constitution. The Headmaster should be the ex-officio president and the senior science teacher the vice-president. One of the pupils may be selected as secretary and another treasurer. All science teachers and pupils will be members. There can also be an executive committee to choke out programmes for the club. A small subscription may be levied from students to meet the current expenditure of the club.

Activities for the Science Club

There cannot be any fixed list of activities. As far as possible these should be based upon the student's interest and aptitudes. The teacher should give varied ideas. The teacher should not force his ideas and interests on his students. Science club activities should remain voluntary. Examples of activities which can be carried out the students are.

(a) Organizing lectures, extension lectures, symposia etc.
(b) Paper reading for the club members on various topics of scientific interest. This will also include project reporting.
(c) Activities relating to the survey of community resource (field trips)
(d) Organizing science exhibitions and participation in science fairs.

Advantages

1. Science club creates a lively and permanent interest in science.
2. They encourage group work which is highly necessary for the advancement of science.
3. They develop social virtues.
4. They after training in leadership and promote self expression. They give the better student an incentive for specialization along lines of individual interests.

12.4. Science Teacher

Introduction

> "Of all the different factors which influence the quality of education and its contribution to national development, the quality, competence and character of teachers are of

> undoubtedly the most significant. Nothing is more important than securing a sufficient supply of high quality results to the teaching profession providing them with the best possible professional preparation and creating satisfactory conditions of work in which they can be fully effective".
>
> —Report of the Education Commission, 1964-66.

The saying 'As the teacher, so the student' very well explains the role of a teacher in the teaching learning process. The main problem which we confront in this connection today is to increase the personal academic and professional efficiency of our teachers. How can it be done? Francis S. Rosecrance gives the following analysis of a competent teacher.

> "He is one whose general liberal education has both breadth and depth. He knows his own areas and knows how learning takes place. He can appraise and help individuals. He is an expert in group process. He possesses skill in methods of teaching, in stimulating thinking, in preserving and extending creativity of his student's skill in making them aware of the values they exhibit and in helping them re-examine those values from time to time".

Professional Equipment

The teacher upon graduation should not consider himself a finished product. He must keep himself informed of the new developments in science and new methods and materials which will make his teaching more effective. Participation in in-service workshops, attending professional meetings, enrolling, in graduate programmes are some of the types of activities which help a teacher to keep abreast of new developments. It is the responsibility of the individual teacher to find the best means to permit him to grow professionally.

The problem of the teaching of science in school is not simply one of what should be taught and how it should be done. The problem of the teacher, is more important, for success or failure of the course rests mainly with him. He may be given an ideal syllabus to work with a well equipped laboratory, library etc. but unless he adds to these a personal enthusiasm and love for his work and a reasonable ability in teaching, his syllabus and equipments will be of no use. A keen well informed teacher with right aims will succeed in spite of difficulties of equipment and similar handicaps. Hence, it is essential that the teacher should be entrusted to those who love the subject and believes in its value.

His knowledge of Subject Matter

> "A teacher can never truly teach unless he is still learning himself. A lamp can never light another lamp unless it continues to its own flame". —Rabindranath Tagore

An efficient teacher of the present world must be a student of pupils as well as a student of subject matter. The teachers should attend refresher courses to revive their enthusiasm and to have some intellectual food and recreation. Educational authorities should arrange lectures and courses for their teachers. These keep the teacher up to date and the temporary change from teacher to student often acts as valuable intellectual topic.

Other ways of keeping the teacher in touch with modern developments and movements include visits to schools and colleges where special features of science are successfully taught and membership of a good library containing important books and publications in all branches of science.

To a beginning science teacher other senior science teachers are valuable sources of information inspiration. Another science teacher can be especially helpful in selecting objectives, methods, materials and sources of information teachers with extensive background in any area of science should be encouraged to do research. They can gain support of their colleagues public and student by publishing his findings in science journals.

The science teacher should cultivate the habit of extensive reading. College Text books are good sources of information for science teachers who want to breadth their knowledge of a particular subject.

The science teacher's breadth of knowledge should be matched by a similar breadth of skills. He should have facility in handling raw materials of wood, metal etc. He has to run laboratory and undertake improvisation and repair of apparatus and equipments.

Science Teachers Club

Science teachers working in the neighbouring schools may organize themselves into a club. Meetings and discussions may be held to improve the curricula, to solve classroom problems etc. The club can provide valuable means of sharing thoughts or methods, activities resources. The inexperienced teachers of science are greatly benefited by such meetings and discussion. The club members may visit industrial undertakings and other places of scientific interest. They can gather much information experience and materials that will help them to improve their teaching.

Duties and Responsibilities of the Science Teacher

The teaching of science presents different problems at different stages. The teachers of young pupils must be ready to answer numerous questions about all sorts of natural phenomena. The teacher of elder students must prepare himself to face the criticism of the mind, approaching maturity. At whatever stage a science master is to teach, it will be necessary for him to have studied the subject for himself to a stage a good deal higher. Teaching of science is not simply passing on accurate scientific information. A teacher's most stimulative teaching will be done only in those fields in which he is himself thinking. A science teacher's thinking will deal with the ways in which young pupils acquire an understanding of nature and with the methods by which they may be encouraged to think accurately about. The science teacher has to arouse love for scientific study in the pupils. This can be done by the exposition of facts, concepts and principles on science using the simplest possible appliances and by bringing the pupils in to contact with the actual experimental work. It is the responsibility of a science teacher to give the pupils training in the scientific method and develop scientific attitudes in them. The teacher should possess curiosity, interest correct attitudes and spirit of scientific enquiry.

The science teacher occupies an important place in the total educational growth of the pupils. The environment in which we live is predominantly coloured by science. The children should be prepared to make adjustments which will result in successful living in complex environment. The science teacher must possess a deep conviction that the experiences he provides to his pupils are vital and will be functional in their contemporary and in later life.

The teacher of science has an exceptional opportunity to observe the pupils in all phases mainly the intellectual manual artistic mechanical, social and creative. He should be able to watch for special aptitudes in each and every pupil so that these may be discovered and developed to their full extent.

The science teacher must be an educational scientist. He should be capable of analyzing new teaching techniques and method conducting of classroom experiments and of seeking new educational materials. It should be remembered that an effective learning situation is seldom possible until the teacher is intimately acquainted with current developments in the fields of science and education.

12.5. Science Exhibitions and Fairs

A science fair, if properly conducted is of great educative value. It may be organized by every school once in year. The various activities of the science fair includes science exhibition arranging lectures, and conducting cultural programmes. Students can be encouraged to take part in science fairs as they help the development of student's personality.

Purpose

1. To focus attention of pupils on science experiments.
2. To stimulate interest in science.
3. To stimulate greater interest in scientific investigations over and above the routine work.
4. To provide a situation for scientific hobby pursuits.
5. To offer an opportunity for the display of scientific talents through exhibits and demonstrations.

Organization

Organization of science fair should be a teacher pupil activity. A committee may be appointed to choke out various activities.

The following factors should be considered while organizing the science fair.

1. *Planning*
   (a) Location

(b) Arrangement for light and water
(c) Furniture
(d) Financial condition
(e) Time for science fair
(f) Proper control and other necessary arrangements

2. *Distribution of work*: Work should be distributed among various committees. There may be an advisory committee, a reception committee, a publicity committee etc.
3. *Judging*: science fair should be judged by an expert team consisting of scientists, heads of departments, professors etc.

   The NCERT has given the following criteria for judging the fair.

   (i) Scientific Approach – 30 points.
   (ii) Originality – 20 points.
   (iii) Technical skill and workmanship – 20 points.
   (iv) Thoroughness – 10 points.
   (v) Dramatic Value – 10 points.
   (vi) Personal interview – 10 points.
4. *Evaluation*: When the fair is over, students and teachers should collectively evaluate it to see the discrepancies and deficiencies so that a better performance can be presented next time.
5. *Advantages of Service Fair*
   (i) Science fairs have social, intellectual, psychological and educational values.
   (ii) The instincts of construction, acquisition, curiosity etc. of children get satisfaction.
   (iii) Students, talents of students are recognized and stimulated.
   (iv) They develop a keen taste and interest for scientific investigation and in solving scientific problems.
   (v) They provide opportunities for encouraging science talent.

13
Creativity in Science Classrooms

In recent times the concept of creativity has gained popularity. The process of identifying talented or creative students and nurturing creativity or developing creativity has been recommended by many educators.

In Indian schools, talented students are being identified and some programmes are organized for them to encourage creative talent in them. Perhaps, much more needs to be done in this direction.

13.1. Meaning of Creativity

Creativity has been defined in different ways by different people. It has been agreed that creativity is a process of an individual producing something unique for himself. Prof. Paul Torrance has defined creativity as follows:

> "I have chosen to define creative thinking as a process of sensing gaps or discovering missing elements, forming ideas or hypotheses and communicating the results, possibly retesting the hypotheses".

Another definition of creative thinking is: "The product has novelty and value for the thinker or the culture; the thinking is unconventional, highly motivated and persistent or of great intensity; the task involves a clear formulation of an initially vague and undefined problem".

It may be useful to generalize that creative thinking involves the highest mental function and the focus is on the creation of useful invention.

Characteristics of Creative Persons

Most of the studies have revealed that creative persons, in a variety of fields, exhibited the same pattern of values and interpersonal relations, including high theoretical and aesthetic values, high self-sufficiency, introversion, greater concern with ideas than with people, and uninterested in social activities. Some of the specific characteristics of creative persons are as follows:

- Challenge assumptions;
- See in new ways;
- Recognize news patterns;
- Make new connections;
- Construct new networks;
- Take risks;
- Take advantage of chance.
- Some other attributes of creative persons are as follows:
- Think originally, flexibly, divergently and imaginatively.
- These persons are able to elaborate.
- These persons are able to improvise, innovate and invent.
- They also exhibit a common pattern of perception and cognition, including preference for complexity, independent judgment, and resistance to group pressure and willingness to take risks.
- Children who were judged creative were humorous in their free association and aspired to unconventional rather than conventional careers.

13.2. Classroom Teaching and Creativity

Development of creativity in the classroom is a significant aspect of classroom interaction where many factors influence the process. A science teacher should know about the process of creativity, means of stimulating and measuring creativity and his own role.

Creative process includes the following four stages:

1. *Preparation:* It is the stage in which a problem is identified and investigated.
2. *Incubation:* It is the stage where ideas are stored below the level of the psyche.

3. *Illumination*: A stage where the solution is suddenly experienced.
4. *Verification*: At this stage new ideas are evaluated.

13.3. Measurement of Creativity

Researchers have agreed that there are five creative abilities namely, fluency, flexibility, originality, elaboration, and sensitivity. These abilities can be measured with the help of tests developed by the researchers. The tests developed by Prof. Paul Torrance and Prof. Baquer Mehendi have been in use.

Research findings have indicated that all persons possess creative talent which can be nurtured as well as measured. These assumptions are as follows:

1. All people possess an element of creativity.
2. Individuals differ considerably in the degree of their creative ability.
3. Freedom to be creative has an effect on mental health.
4. Suitable environment gives chance to become creative.
5. Overuse of positive reinforcement is not good for the growth of creativity.
6. A creative person has sensitivity to situations.

Stimulating Creativity in the Classroom

Researchers have suggested many acts to encourage creativity in the classroom. Some of the suggestions are as follows:

1. Students should get a variety of learning situations to solve the problems.
2. Problem solving or discovery approach should be encouraged in the classroom.
3. Thought provoking questions should be asked in the classroom to stimulate thinking among the students.
4. Students should be encouraged to practise risk taking abilities, independent judgement, and self-assured actions.
5. Science teachers should create an awareness of the role of sub-consciousness.
6. They should provide experiences with mind stretching exercises.

7. Students should get an opportunity to increase sensitivity.
8. They should be helped by science teachers to understand why they engage in various exercises related to creative thinking.

In Indian school situation, it is the responsibility of the science teacher to provide responsive learning environment, where students get freedom to work independently and solve problems through divergent thinking. A science teacher can utilize science club as a place which stimulates self learning and students can pursue projects of their own choice.

13.4. Values in Science Education

The National Policy on Education – 1986 has observed that there is erosion of essential values and the increasing dynamism in society has brought to focus the need for readjustments in curriculum in order to make education a forceful tool for the cultivation of social and moral values. Education as an organized social system has an important function in the development of moral, spiritual and aesthetic values. In science classroom too, a science teacher cannot avoid dealing with values. Each science teacher in his teaching communicates values concepts to his students directly or indirectly. The important question is to deal consciously with values in the classroom.

Definition of Values

Every society is sustained by a core of 'universals' – elements of culture which all people know, believe, use and do and which represent the society's ideals or norms. The heart of the universals are the values or the rules by which people order their social existence. The choice of proper living, mutual respect and independent thinking depends on the values which people cherish. In Indian context, such values should encourage democratic values, national integration, secularism, objectivity, rationality and the development of nationalism.

There are many definition of them term 'value'. Shaver and Strong have given the following definitions:

"Values are our standards and principles for judging worth.

> *They are the criteria by which we judge people, objects, ideas, actions and situations to be good, worthwhile, desirable; or on the other hand, bad, worthless, despicable, or of course, somewhere in between these extremes".*

Values may also be defined as

- a directive factor in human behaviour;
- a standard held by individuals or groups.

Bond describes value as "an assertable belief about the worth, goodness, preferability of an object, event, idea, act, or other phenomenon, by valuation. In other words, determining the goodness or worth of phenomenon".

Education and the Spirit of Science has mentioned values of science. Some of these are as follows:

- Questioning of all things.
- Respect for logic.
- Consideration of premise.
- Consideration of consequences.

In scientific work most important values are objectivity, rationality, honesty, readiness to change the opinion in the light of new evidences, humility and the development of scientific temper.

13.5. Value Education

Value education involves developing a sensitivity to values. In a traditional way values may be developed by setting examples, through persuasion, through inspiration and by establishing rules and regulations. The most appropriate approach in the classroom should be through questions which are open-ended in nature, require divergent thinking and open discussion. It is environment of home and school which also influences values.

Value aspect of an individual is a complex aspect and it needs an all-out effort in cognitive, affective and psychomotor domains. In other words, knowledge aspect is not sufficient in itself. It should be added with feelings, attitude, emotions and interests.

The science teacher should lay emphasis on experimentation,

discussion and inquiry learning. Individual and small group project work will also help in developing scientific values. Panel discussion, educational tours and awareness about the science related social issues will build a value system among the students.

The science teacher should crate environment where students start getting awareness about the scientific temper, scientific work and respect for logic and reason. Presenting concrete examples from the work and biographies of scientists will be of great help. Peer group, mass media and T.V. also help in developing values.

Jerome Kagan and Jean Piaget have written that the child's sense of values and morality begins to take shape in the months just before his second birthday. Perhaps, work of Jean Piaget and Lawrence Kohl will be of some help to science teachers in understanding the value system.

14
E-Learning

14.1. Theoretical Foundation

The intimate relationship between the private and shared worlds is highlighted because e-learning has been most often used to provide more efficient delivery of information and, thus, favour independent learning. The nature of this dominant application is a serious limiting condition to the full utilization of the capabilities of e-learning. While autonomy and access to information are not inherently disadvantageous, there is little recognition of either the transactional nature of an educational experience or of e-learning to support collaborative asynchronous learning. It is the technical capability of e-learning's unique ability to bring together a community of learners, unrestricted by time or place, that must be understood. From this perspective, e-learning would appear to offer the means of creating an educational experience so long idealized in educational theory.

Dewey (1938) identified two principles that are reflected in the theoretical framework developed here. One is 'interaction', which unifies the subjective (personal) and objective (social) worlds in an immediate timeframe. Through this interaction, ideas are generated that illuminate the eternal world. That is, meaning is constructed and shared. Through interaction, ideas are communicated and knowledge is constructed and confirmed. The second principle is 'continuity', which goes to the importance of creating the foundation for future learning. As Dewey stated, 'the result of the educative process is capacity for further education' (1916: 68), which has great value for both the individual and society.

Dewey would have embraced the choice and diversity of e-learning with its opportunity for 'active inquiry' and the 'individual variations' it provides; however, he would have also been adamant that discipline required to elevate the process to 'reflective inquiry' be brought to bear on the information. E-learning and the Internet are wonderful sources of ideas, but to be 'genuinely educative' they must provide an experience that assures 'continuity' or the foundation for new, worthwhile learning experiences.

Education is fundamentally an interactive or transactional process. The challenges and confusion surrounding control issues go to the normative role and responsibility afforded the teacher. It is the teacher who has the legitimate responsibility to define the curriculum and design the educational activities. Unfortunately, there is little opportunity for collaboration in the planning process. That is, the student has little input or influence in planning the process or expected outcomes of the educational experience. This creates the contradictory situation where the student is expected to assume responsibility for activities and an outcome over which they have little input.

The solution inherent to the transactional perspective is to give students opportunities for dialogue regarding outcome expectations learning activities, and means of assessment. While some aspects of the educational transaction may not be open for negotiation, it is important that students share in this understanding. By being included in the larger process, and being provided choice where appropriate, students are given a sense of control and, therefore, take responsibility for the quality of the educational outcome.

The transactional perspective on teaching and learning reflects a dynamic balance of responsibility and control issues congruent with the educational purpose and the capabilities of the students. E-learning draws attention to fundamental responsibility and control issues.

14.2. The Technology of E-Learning

The intimate relationship between the private and shared worlds is highlighted because e-learning has been most often used to provide more efficient delivery of information and thus, favour independent learning. The nature of this dominant application is a serious limiting condition to the full utilization of the capabilities of e-learning. While autonomy and access to information are not inherently disadvantageous, there is little recognition of either the transactional nature of an educational experience or of e-learning to support collaborative asynchronous learning. It is the technical capability of e-learning's unique ability to bring together a community of learners, unrestricted by time or place, that must be understood. From this perspective, e-learning would appear to offer the means of creating an educational experience so long idealized in educational theory.

14.3. Benefits of E-Learning

The educational system of today needs to impart to all learners three new foundational skills: to make learning a relevant and lifelong process—a process of continuous growth change and evolution and adaptation. The schools of the twentieth century were clustered around the idea that time would be constant and learning would be variable. Today with computers taking over, jobs that can be done with minimum education are fast diminishing.

The idea of schools as a fixed time activity is being replaced by the concept of continuous learning built around a variety of tools and techniques. The twenty-first century classroom will be wherever the learner is located—at school, on the bus ride home, in the park, at a museum, or in the playground. Traditional tools will co-exist with the hi-tech tools of the telematic era. (telematics is the integration of information and communication technologies).

The teacher's role in this distributed setting is to be quite different from that of content presenter and test giver. The teacher in this setting will operate in a system based on four components: campfires, watering holes, caves, and life. The campfire is the informational space associated with lectures and other methods of direct instruction. The watering hole is the conversational space occupied when learners converse among themselves or with their teachers about a particular topic. The cave is the conceptual space where ideas are developed in relative solitude and where student projects are designed and built. Life is the contextual space where the things have been learned and are applied in the world outside of school.

Learning has always taken place in these four spaces, yet twentieth century schools often failed to provide the right balance and learning suffered as a result. These four learning spaces provide a framework for the community at large that can envision educational opportunity. Flexibility is the key for the effective definition of the roles. Technology can become the force that equalizes the educational opportunities of children regardless of location and social and economic circumstances.

The internet eliminates geography as a limiting factor. A child in a remote hamlet can have the same access to the same reference materials as one located in the cosmopolitan city. Time is transcended by telematic tools. Technology will have an increasingly positive impact on the student's creativity. Access to multiple expressive modalities is important.

Educators are also great beneficiaries of the telematic revolution. It opens up new opportunities for casual dialogues on a wide range of topics, and helps overcome the sense of isolation sometimes felt by educators whose areas of interest have few local enthusiasts. In addition to conversing with peers, communication with learners, their parents, the community at large is facilitated with the same tools. Though technology promises the panacea to better learning, sales hungry decision makers have exploited it. Now it is faced with the challenge of maintaining the delicate balance between quality and quantity.

Society has been credited with creating technology, but technology is simultaneously creating society. These observations would also suggest that technology is beginning to exercise a benevolent tyranny over humankind. People have become compulsive information consumers who favour the passive reaction of information as a form of entertainment over the more challenging act of thinking.

Maintaining quality presupposes building a code of ethics to the telematic infrastructure, just as science without responsibility is like a sword without a sheaths; so too, telematic education without ethics will lead to gross debasement of human energies. The ethic values to bear in mind cannot be isolated from human values and responsibilities. It should also provide built-in evaluation that protect internal human ecological aspects. Primarily quality check must respect human rights to privacy, to avoid intrusion and abuse of these rights, and to avoid placing all information on equal levels.

14.4. Web Based Learning

Effective web-based learning should include not just training in the use of technology. It must be integrated with pedagogical uses of technology to bring about learning for the development of lifelong learning skills and other emerging goals of education to meet the demands of the information age. Whenever web technology is used in educational settings, it is vital to reflect on how this affects students, faculty members, courses and institutions.

Web-based learning is seen by many as a transformative vehicle for increasing the pace of change and reform in higher education. For these and other reasons, analysis of quality assurance in web-based learning is an essential topic for education policy makers. The common problem now in the higher education sector is to identify an effective model to assure quality in the delivery of web-based learning that can fit the various stakeholders' expectations. The first stage for doing this is to identify the critical success factors that would contribute to quality assurance in web-based learning.

As the use of technology to facilitate and deliver distance learning courses has increased, new challenges have emerged for the administration, faculty, staff and students of universities developing and implementing distance learning programmes. Many faculties fear distance learning is just a means of reducing their ranks, or a means to solve budget problems. Others fear the dehumanisation and alienation of students as well as loss of critical thinking and social skills. On the other hand, rather than feeling threatened, the faculty should embrace distance learning as a way for more students to access their courses, resulting in a greater intellectual audience and less chance of a course being cancelled due to low enrolment.

The web profoundly influences society in general and universities in particular. One of the consequences of this tremendous surge in online communication has been the rapid growth of technology-mediated distance learning at the higher education level.

This extraordinary growth of technology-mediated distance learning in higher education has prompted several different agencies to develop principles, guidelines, or benchmarks to ensure quality distance education. The web is a major technological advancement reshaping not only our society but also that of universities worldwide. In the light of this, universities have to capitalise on the web for both teaching and learning, and one progressive development of this is the use of web-based learning in distance education settings. The benchmarks for quality assurance of web-based learning were considered important, and in general the participated institutions strove to incorporate them into their policies, practices and procedures.

At the same time, there were few benchmarks that did not enjoy consensus among the academic members, and in some instances were not even considered mandatory to ensure quality for web-based learning. In order to have an effective quality assurance model for web-based learning, it will need to, conduct study on students' perception on this issue, and incorporate the results with the perception of academic staff to form a more complete picture of the whole quality assurance model.

Each quality assurance system needs to be careful in analysing the situation of the specific institution. It needs to be very flexible in its approach, and the combination of process and technology needs to be carefully considered, as unintended consequences in one area can originate from a bad choice in another. It may be worth noting that a firm adherence to an explicit view of what constitutes good web-based learning, and an explicit view of issues of change and culture will furthermore influence the specific approach taken in assuring the quality web-based learning.

For education, broadband access means the elimination of time and distance from the learning equation. Broadband carries with it powerful multimedia learning opportunities, the full interactivity of instructional content, and the quality and speed of communications. Wireless solutions may enable underdeveloped and remote areas to quickly take advantage of the web via wireless phones, two-way pagers, and hand-held devices.

During this period, internet access in households has grown dramatically. In just a year and a half the share of households with internet access doubled, rising from 26.2% to 41.5%. Rural households are catching up. Home access is important for students doing research, taking online courses and communicating with other teachers and other learners. For parents, online access means new kinds of communication with their children's schools, with their children's teachers and with other parents.

For all households, internet access is another way to connect with their communities and government services. Home access helps to advance economic opportunities: low-income users were the most likely to display using the internet to look for jobs. Those learners without internet access at home rely on schools, libraries, and other public places to provide this access. For many economically disadvantaged and minority group youngsters, a computer at school or in the library after school is the only link to the wide world of the internet. Educational institutions are struggling to provide students with internet access, and great strides have been made in bringing schools, libraries, and postsecondary institutions online.

Post-secondary education institutions are also rapidly expanding student access to the internet. The internet is a double-edged sword for these learners. It can be a gateway to new opportunities, or a barrier that challenges them even further. Web-based learning environments can provide support and challenge through multiple means of:

(i) Representation (e.g., a math concept in both text and graphic modes; animated science simulations; poetry read aloud by the author, etc.)

(ii) Expression (i.e., use of text; sound; images; video; and combinations of media as vehicles for expressive literacy through writing, illustrating, speaking, video-making, and drawing)

(iii) Engagement to attract the easily bored or the easily distracted learner. Designing accessibility into an internet site or a course at the beginning is far less expensive than after the fact. Designs that create barriers harm everyone, not just people with disabilities.

Teachers are the key to effective use of web-based tools and applications, but first they must become skilled at using them. It is the teacher, after all, who guides instruction and shapes the instructional context in which the internet and other technologies are used. It is a teacher's skill at this, more than any other factor, that determines the degree to which students learn from their Internet experiences.

Teachers must be comfortable with technology, able to apply

it appropriately, and conversant with new technological tools, resources, and approaches. If all the pieces are put into place, teachers should find that they are empowered to advance their own professional skills through these tools as well.

While younger teachers may have basic technology skills they realise that they, like their older colleagues, do not know how to apply these skills to teaching. The ability to use technology for non-instructional purposes does not necessarily translate into either the will or the capability to use technology to support student learning. Although they are not technophobes, these new teachers lack a clear conception of effective classroom uses of technology in their subject area.

Professional development is the critical ingredient for effective use of technology in the classroom. Seventy per cent of educators polled regarding technology in instruction put professional development at the top of their list of technology challenges. Professional development is often called 'training', but the term implies much more than just building basic technology skills. It means developing a vision built on the understanding that technology is a tool that can offer solutions to longstanding teaching and learning problems.

Fortunately, the internet is making it possible to connect teachers to each other, giving opportunities for mentoring, collaboration, and formal and informal online learning. Through the internet, teachers have access to high quality online professional development opportunities beyond what the local school or district is able to offer. And, in working in online environments, teachers obtain a collateral benefit: they learn important technological skills.

In short, a supportive social structure is one of the key elements for successful online learning. But unless new teachers enter the classroom ready to teach with technology, students will never catch up with modern technology. If teacher education programmes do not address this issue head on, they lose the opportunity to get it right with a whole generation of new teachers and the students they teach.

The intimate relationship between the private and shared worlds is highlighted because e-learning has been most often used to provide more efficient delivery of information and, thus, favour independent learning. The nature of this dominant application is a serious limiting condition to the full utilization of the capabilities of e-learning. While autonomy and access to information are not inherently disadvantageous, there is little recognition of either the transactional nature of an educational experience or of e-learning to support collaborative asynchronous learning. It is the technical capability of e-learning's unique ability to bring together a community of learners, unrestricted by time or place, that must be understood. From this perspective, e-learning would appear to offer the means of creating an educational experience so long idealized in educational theory.

Dewey (1938) identified two principles that are reflected in the theoretical framework developed here. One is 'interaction', which unifies the subjective (personal) and objective (social) worlds in an immediate timeframe. Through this interaction, ideas are generated that illuminate the eternal world. That is, meaning is constructed and shared. Through interaction, ideas are communicated and knowledge is constructed and confirmed. The second principle is 'continuity', which goes to the importance of creating the foundation for future learning. As Dewey stated, '*the result of the educative process is capacity for further education*' (1916: 68), which has great value for both the individual and society.

Dewey would have embraced the choice and diversity of e-learning with its opportunity for 'active inquiry' and the 'individual variations' it provides; however, he would have also been adamant that discipline required to elevate the process to 'reflective inquiry' be brought to bear on the information. E-learning and the Internet are wonderful sources of ideas, but to be 'genuinely educative' they must provide an experience that assures 'continuity' or the foundation for new, worthwhile learning experiences.

Education is fundamentally an interactive or transactional process. The challenges and confusion surrounding control issues go to the normative role and responsibility afforded the teacher. It is the teacher who has the legitimate responsibility to define the curriculum and design the educational activities. Unfortunately, there is little opportunity for collaboration in the planning process. That is, the student has little input or influence in planning the process or expected outcomes of the educational experience. This creates the contradictory situation where the student is expected to assume responsibility for activities and an outcome over which they have little input.

The solution inherent to the transactional perspective is to give students opportunities for dialogue regarding outcome expectations learning activities, and means of assessment. While some aspects of the educational transaction may not be open for negotiation, it is important that students share in this understanding. By being included in the larger process, and being provided choice where appropriate, students are given a sense of control and, therefore, take responsibility for the quality of the educational outcome.

The transactional perspective on teaching and learning reflects a dynamic balance of responsibility and control issues congruent with the educational purpose and the capabilities of the students. E-learning draws attention to fundamental responsibility and control issues.

14.5. Teaching and Learning through WEB

Emergent forms of education will expand educational technology beyond current conceptions of flexible delivery. A three-stage model that highlights the maturity of flexible learning initiatives, from flexible delivery through flexible interaction to flexible exploration can be envisaged. The majority of current educational technology implementations fit into the first stage and very few reach the third stage. Consequently, the three levels can be represented as a pyramid, highlighting the present focus on lower level activities and the need to progress to higher level activities.

The first stage, flexible delivery, embraces the majority of current Web-based delivery efforts. The second stage, flexible interaction, supports a more cooperative form of flexible delivery by using Web and Internet technologies to enable students to interact outside traditional boundaries. Many course Web sites already utilise bulletin board and chat facilities. However, this is often an adjunct to the learning process and simply continues the information delivery notion. Movement from the first level to the second implies a more conscious utilization of synchronous and asynchronous communication devices to engage students in both lecturer-to-student and peer-to-peer investigations of problems being explored. The third stage is characterised by student exploration of concepts using Web and Internet technologies. At this stage, students can explore concepts in a non-linear, student-directed fashion. They can, in effect, design their own learning experiences. For the most part, little effort has been expended at this level.

The emergent forms of education, situated in the diversity/ collaboration quadrant, encompass the flexible interaction and flexible exploration stages. These are summarised below:

14.6. Flexible Interaction

If we accept that effective teaching and learning involve a process of developing and changing individuals' values and beliefs, enabling them to see the world from a different perspective, then it is appropriate to view the educational process as complicated layers of social interaction. But, no matter which definition of teaching and learning we subscribe to, a high level of student-student or student-teacher interaction is inevitable. The Web and the Internet offer a wide array of opportunities to support student interaction. The facilities range from the simple bulletin board, ICQ, IRC, and other generic chat facilities to the more sophisticated online tutorial facilities like Net Meeting, white Pine's Meeting Point and Class Point, and Lotus's Learning Space. Web-based course were products like Web CT, Top Class, College, and Blackboard's Course Site, which offer interactive facilities, are increasingly being used. However, recent surveys have shown that communication facilities, alone will not deliver increased value to students or academics (Parry, Cockroft, Breton, Abernethy, & Gillies, 1999; Vargo & Craff, 1999). It is not the technology itself, but the way it is integrated into the learning process that creates value for students.

An example of an integrated learning process using Web and Internet technologies is the virtual collaborative team room. Traditional project groups often base themselves around a team room- a physical location where material related to the project can be grouped together in a work environment. As a collaboration tool, the physical team room is often highly effective. Group members are able to enter the room and begin working by themselves on a particular piece of the project, and then easily adapt themselves to working in groups should another member arrive. Further, due to its ability to develop project memory, the physical team room facilities group members to pick up where another member left off on a particular task, thereby allowing for time-diverse collaboration. But the physical team room requires the co-location of all members of the project group. An alternative is to create a virtual team room utilising group applications. By locating the team room within an Internet-connected computer system, group members are able to participate in the project, and obtain many of the advantages of the physical team room even if they are in geographically diverse locations (Davis, Motteram, Crock & Mitchell, 1999).

14.7. Flexible Exploration

Flexible Exploration focuses on students as active constructors of knowledge (Brown, 1994). Practically this is reflected in the widespread adoption of case-based and problem problem-based learning approaches to student learning (Bentley, Lowry & Sandy, 1999; Prawat, 1993). One of the perceived advantages of these methods is that they allow students to deal with complex realistic situations, to gain experience in practical decision-making and to develop their own models and approaches for dealing with unstructured problems (Bentley, Lowry & Sandy, 1999). It is claimed that student recall and understanding of key concepts is improved when they are actively engaged in such realistic learning activities (Mills–Jones, 1999).

The loss of richness in the material is commonly a product of tight teaching schedules or attempts to highlight the lecturer's perception of the important aspects of the case. As a result, students tend to approach the case as an exercise in re-organising the material to find the answer. This reduces both the experiential and realism aspects of the learning exercise (Bentley, Lowry & Sandy, 1999; Friedman & Khan, 1994; Gallagher, 1994). The internet and the Web offer a range of opportunities to address these concerns, particularly in terms of increased realism, improved student motivation, and an increased emphasis on self-directed student exploration of the material. At the simplest level multimedia facilities can enhance the visual aspect of case material. Audio and video tools can be sued to upgrade case exhibits and break up the written components of the material. This is often enough to improve student motivation to explore the case material on their own or with peer groups.

In teaching cases specifically developed to take advantage of new technologies, communications tools and simple artificial intelligence agents can be used to encourage student interaction with the virtual actors in the case. Controlled interaction with artificial organisational units like steering committees or management groups can be supported allowing students to explore the material in ways not originally conceived by the lecturer. The student experience can also be enhanced by the ability to contextualise the case material within the wider context of resources available on the Web. These features all add to the complexity and realism of the problem being explored.

The following may be considered good principles for the design and development of effective educational technology systems to support emergent teaching practices.

1. *Support appropriate curriculum goals and objectives:* Educational technology needs to be developed to support educationally derived objectives and goals. This necessitates detailed exploration of how each technological mechanism supports learning in specific higher education contexts. Well-designed educational technology should allow multiple teaching goals to be realised. For a system to be widely useful and broadly accepted, it needs to fulfil a variety of educational objectives and student needs. The most important design question for educational technology is probably whether the system should be developed at all.
2. *Contextualise learning:* The use of new technologies offers the opportunity to contextualise learning in ways not previously possible. The use of on-line systems and simulators allow for student exploration of knowledge domains within a frame work resembling actual practice. It is particularly important that technology does not de-contextualise learning by conveying mixed messages.
3. *Create communities of self-directed learners*: Interactive communication facilities are of value only when they create communities of learners and not when they simply provide additional avenues of information delivery. Well-designed technology-based systems also ensure that students progress in their learning activities, while

allowing them to broaden their understanding and explore tangents if they wish. One of the strengths of emergent educational technology is its ability to broaden students' conceptions of the world. Pop quizzes are useful tools, animations can engage, and discussion forums can support communication, but none of these by Good educational technology should not promote rote learning but encourage exploration, thinking, and problem solving.

4. *Encourage and facilitate open discourse:* Many existing technology-based educational systems are designed simply to provide a more flexible method for the delivery of existing teaching material. But traditional face-to-face delivery allows students the chance for social learning not automatically present in technology-mediated delivery. In traditional delivery, students meet together in class and in small groups as they walk to or from class. In these groups students may talk about such things as their reactions to material or to assignments, and work load copying strategies. New educational technology also needs to provide facilities which encourage and allow interaction between students and teachers. This discourse should, where possible, be removed from the limitations of time and location constraints.
5. *Provide appropriate feedback channels:* Much of the existing educational technology allows only for one-way communication of material. It is important, in conjunction with the previous principles, that emergent systems allow for teachers to support and monitor student learning through the provision of appropriate feedback. This feedback is an important aspect of any students' performance and perceived self-efficacy (which in turn affects future performance). The feedback should go beyond traditional communication of results and assessment feedback and incorporate more feedback that supports, challenges, and motivates students
6. *Support teaching and learning needs:* When educational technology is developed from a purely pedagogical perspective, it is likely to support student needs. However, it is important that emergent systems also support teachers' needs. A system's 'success' is highly questionable

if it creates extra burdens for teachers or removes those aspects of teaching that are considered enjoyable. A good system should enhance a teacher's participation with students and support other teaching-related issues like satisfaction, motivation, and career concerns.

7. *Engage Students:* Badly designed educational technology can create a gulf between students and teachers, increasing student alienation and reducing their learning capacity. In these circumstances, it is likely that there will be resistance to technology use. It is possible to overcome fear of technology by supporting a variety of learning experiences and by providing choice in learning approaches. Well- designed systems should enhance a student's perception of self-efficacy and not detract from it Educational technology should in their students and not create a perception of distance.
8. *Be accurate, adaptable and flexible:* Good educational systems can be costly, complex, and difficult to create and maintain. It is important that anticipated benefits are not negated by poor instructions, simple errors, and technology failings. Systems must be adaptable so that teachers can ensure currency of the material provided. It is also important that they be flexible to allow teachers to adapt the teaching practices to suit different student groupings and learners to adapt them to their individual learning styles. The need for structure in a technology must not remove a student's ability to self-regulate their learning experience.

Web can have a profound effect on course delivery, particularly in relation to developing delivery mechanisms capable of meeting the individual needs of diverse student cohorts. As students become more informed and ICT capabilities develop, there is a need for better-designed educational technology that supports teaching practices rather than acts as a bill board advertising technological wonder.

Our thinking on flexible learning is influenced by our belief in a multi-staged approach to flexible learning, built on the foundations of constructivism and social interactionism. The advantages of constructivism lie in the emphasis on learning as a process of sense-making through experience. Learning under these modes is active and reflective techniques which have been proven to increase understanding and retention. Good ICTs offer many opportunities for students to become active, reflective, self-directed learners. The goals of education technology must be to support truly flexible forms of education, improve opportunities for learning, and cater for different learning styles. Distance learning in disguise will not result in long-term benefits to students and teachers. The key lesson we have learned from our development and assessment of educational technology over the last few years is that educational technology produced without a clear pedagogical foundation rarely results in improved student learning. Finally, the point must be made that educational technology should not be considered a focal point for educational reform but rather a resource to be integrated into a wide repertoire of educational resources.

14.8. Learning to Learn Online

Students are, for the most part, unaware of the demands that online learning will place on them as learners. They generally enter an online class with con- traditional expectations, that is, that the instructor will "teach" and they will "learn" from the material the instructor provides. They do not know that the instructor is less visible in the learning process and that the instructor role is one of facilitator rather than of traditional teacher or lecturer. They also have not been told that the online learning process is less structured and demands significantly more input from them as learners to make it successful. Consequently, it is important that the instructor convey this information to students prior to beginning an online course. Many times difficulties emerge when students have differing sets of expectations from the course and the instructor and little or no attempt is made to clarify expectations at the outset.

Students generally enter an online program with the expectation that a course will be more attuned to their needs as learners. This may mean that the course is more convenient for them due to distance or work and family demands. Or it may mean that they do not like large classroom situations and prefer the potential for increased instructor-student interaction.

Because students enter online programs and courses with

expectations that might not match the realities of online learning, some institutions are course creating online courses to teach students about online learning, and some are even mandating that students complete an introductory course before embarking on other online classes. Some incorporate mandatory face-to face orientations to online programs and courses, involving both computer training and training in what it means to learn online and how to be an effective online student. The assumption behind all of these approaches is the same: To maximize the educational potential for both the online classroom – and online students. We must pay attention to teaching our teachers how to teach and teaching our learners how to learn when teaching and learning are virtual.

As with faculty training, conducting student training online allows students to experience online learning before they take an actual course. Regardless of the means by which the training is conducted, the following should be included in a student orientation to online learning:

The basics of logging on to the Internet including the use of a browser,

- accessing the course site,
- using course management software,
- saving and printing material found online and
- basic Internet searching, and E-mail.

Understanding what is required to become successful online learner including time requirements and time management.

The differences between a face-to-face course and an online course, including the role of the instructor and the roles of students as well as expectations about how students will be evaluated.

Interaction between the instructor and students and among students can be ensured.

How to Give Feedback to Other Students

Providing an orientation course might not resolve all of the issues for students as they make the transition to the online classroom. But it certainly can help to provide a clearer understanding of the differences in the type of educational experience they are about to undertake and can help to clarify expectations. Following up with a written guide to online work, whether in hard copy or placed on the institution's Web site, can help to reinforce this learning. When concerns or complaints regarding expectations arise, students can then be referred back to the guidelines that are readily available to them to help them understand the online teaching and learning methods and processes.

If the institution cannot provide student training about how to learn, then suggestions for how to learn online become the responsibility of the faculty who are delivering courses. Ways in which faculty can orient students include the following:

- Hold a face-to-face, hands-on orientation, if possible, to show students the course site and discuss online learning.
- Provide an orientation to the course on the course site or as a first discussion item.
- Provide students with a list of frequently asked questions and responses to those questions.
- Place basic information about how to navigate the course site on the welcome screen or course home page.
- Send an e-mail message to each student enrolled in the course containing orientation information. (Palloff & Pratt, 2001, p. 43)

14.9. Interactive Learning

Interactivity is one of the attractive components of web-based education and is not limited to the use of hypertext and the media. When talking about interactivity, we should refer not so much to interaction with learning material that someone has made available on the network or on CD-ROM, but rather to human-machine interaction governed by software, or, better still, personal interaction mediated by network technology.

Even when using the technology's potential to the fullest, there is no guarantee about the quality that interaction will bring to the learning process. The development of new technology, especially over the past decade, has led to the production of multimedia material of high quality, at least in aesthetic terms. Looking at these products from the communication viewpoint, we can identify two extremes. At one end, there are products with a low level of i which tend to reproduce the traditional lecture format.

Another type of interactivity is direct interactivity between individuals, where the technology does not "drive" but acts as a passive mediator. This is the case with computer networks. While interactivity is no guarantee of quality, social interaction with peers or with one's trainers plays a key role in the learning process, both from the psychosocial and psycho-affective viewpoints. In this sense, ICT services can make an enormous contribution. Despite this, there is still a general trend in distance education toward one-way schemes.

Interaction is imperative if the quality of the process is to be raised: interaction with materials, between students and their tutors/teachers, as well as between all the participants. Information technology and, more importantly, computer communication technology can play a vital role in fostering this interaction, even if use of these means is not in itself a guarantee of higher quality. As is usually the case, a fundamental role is played by course designers and coordinators, who have the means to steer the process toward the predefined goals.

However, raising interactivity in the process either involves investing in multimedia products which are very complex and expensive, or entails increasing the amount of online tutoring. Courseware tools also have been developed over the past few years to aid in the development of electronic learning environments by integrating access to information, interactivity, and synchronous and asynchronous communication.

Human infrastructure is the foundation of student learning, and physical, technological, and human elements must be integrated. Human infrastructure is critical to total institutional infrastructure; technology is impacting not only physical infrastructure but human infrastructure as well. As new teaching-learning paradigms evolve, the faculty must be strengthened through training and university supports. Investment in the development of faculty will build the human infrastructure essential to technology-driven higher education.

The web is not an interactive tool unless elements are incorporated to promote that interaction. The development of WBI, however, requires an even higher level of understanding. Engaging in WBI requires not only the instructor or developer to have a level of expertise in WBI but the student as well. Both must possess a level of knowledge or aptitude enabling them to perform the basic operations of both the computer hardware and system software. Both must be able to apply simple problem solving techniques as well as have a general understanding or foundation in how to navigate the WWW and use functions such as e-mail and/or fax.

The remote student in WBI will also need access to the same student services as on-campus students, such as registration, tuition payment, student support, examinations, and library services. Creating WBI without marketing and promoting the availability of course work deflates the potential profitability that increased enrolment can offer. It also prevents meeting the identified need. If the department or university does not have an individual or group of individuals designated to promote web-based courses, marketing efforts will become a faculty responsibility.

The development of an online syllabus and readings could be the entrance into WBI, followed by the incorporation of hyperlinks and the addition of text and image-based instructional materials. Professors are currently creating web pages for courses, syllabi, readings, and links. E-mail may initially serve as the primary mode of communication, followed by the incorporation of a listserv, then synchronous chats.

14.10. Adaptive Learning Systems

Some of the fundamental elements contributing to adaptive learning are described below.

Learning Objects

For years, the e-learning industry has anticipated the day when learners could personalize, assemble on the fly, and access e-learning on demand. Development teams would be able to build content a single time, store it electronically, reuse it, and deploy it in different formats with a simple button click. A small content piece—a learning object—would establish the foundation upon which these capabilities rest.

At its most basic level, a learning object is a piece of content that's smaller than a course or lesson. But the learning object doesn't exist in a vacuum; it's one of three interdependent components:

- the learning object itself
- metatagging, or the standardized way to describe the content in code
- a *Learning Content Management System* (LCMS) that stores, tracks, and delivers content.

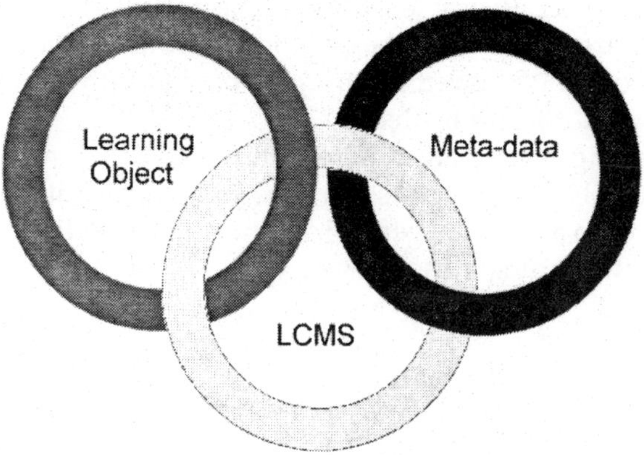

LCMS vendors and other learning object evangelists promise that when you combine those three components, the organization, developers, and the learner benefit.

Content developers benefit because they can build content once and reuse it in several courses and delivery media, and they can search for and use content that other developers have built and stored in the database.

The organization benefits because it's able to

- develop and deploy learning content quickly and efficiently
- port content easily between multiple LMSs or LCMSs
- reduce content development and delivery costs
- reduce maintenance time and costs.

Finally, the learner benefits because he or she can access

- individualized learning paths
- competency-based rather than course-based learning events

- content that has been adapted to his or her individual learning style
- immediate, just-in-time, just-enough performance support.

The Elusive Object

Learning object. Reusable learning object. Reusable information object. Shareable content object. Modular building block. Chunk. Nugget. Lego. Whatever. The list goes on, but each term is simply a synonym for learning object.

Learning objects are different things to different e-learning professionals. In fact, there seem to be as many definitions as there are people to ask. But in general, learning object definitions cover the following categories:

- *content:* a learning objective, the content and learning activities supporting that objective, and the assessment that's mapped to the learning objective
- *size or seat time*: a chunk of learning that takes no longer than 15 minutes to complete
- *context and capabilities:* a nugget of learning that can exist stand alone and be delivered to a learner on an as-needed, just-in-time, just-enough basis
- *tagging and storage:* a piece of content that's described with a standardized set of meta-tags.

The LCMS: Object Creation, Storage, and Delivery

Storing small objects in a database is nothing new. In the systems development and engineering fields, the object paradigm is used to manage large things. In general, the smaller the stored items, the more numerous the opportunities to reuse, track, and combine them. But to the training industry, electronic object storage and reusability are new concepts that have ushered in a new tool that turns course-based content development on its head—the LCMS.

A typical LCMS offers the following capabilities: content authoring or assembly, content management, workflow management, content storage, and content delivery. Most LCMSs store content in an XML database, but deliver it in HTML for Web browsers. Many are capable of delivering the content to other media, such as CD-ROM and print.

What benefits do LCMSs offer? You create and store content once, but deliver it many times, often simultaneously to different users. And the database stores content separately from presentation, which enables publishing of the exact same content in different formats.

A standardized learning object would adopt a particular learning theory and respond to a set of business requirements. As a result, all learning content entered into a standards-compliant LCMS would follow the same instructional philosophy and have similar functionality to support it. But that's not good for learners or the industry. Instead, LCMS vendors have based their learning object definitions on different learning theories and individual cases.

From an instructional standpoint, Chapman identifies two learning object categories: prescriptive and adaptive. By far, prescriptive learning objects are the most common among LCMS vendors. Prescriptive learning objects focus on structure. In other words, all learning objects in that LCMS adhere to a particular instructional design structure and granularity. By contrast, adaptive learning objects focus on learners and can change according to the learner's profile and shifting needs.

Adapting to Learning Styles

For example, Adaptive Tutoring Systems of Toronto, Canada, employs an adaptive learning object design. Its LCMS redefines a learning object on the fly, as the system monitors individual learner performance and adapts to an individual's learning style. President Bruce Miner says, "Our adaptive technology focuses on the learning style and context of the student. We ask, *How does the student learn best?* Then, we render the content that fits that style."

Adaptive Tutoring Systems uses artificial intelligence technology to track a learner's performance and preferences, continually update user profiles, and deliver learning objects accordingly. Developers save time and money by creating one learning object that addresses several learning styles. They don't need to create a different learning object for each learning style. For example, as the artificial intelligence system adapts to a visual learner, that learner will receive less text on the screen and will see graphics emphasized.

Also, the ATS system can deliver learning object content appropriate to the user's bandwidth, for example, reducing the video frame rate for learners with modems. "All this [bandwidth delivery] information sits inside the learning object," says Miner.

Competencies and Learning Objects

Generation 21's LCMS, Total Knowledge Management, falls into the prescriptive learning object category. But don't let the prescriptive tag fool you. TKM does allow some flexibility in design and delivery.

TKM specifies a content hierarchy, in which smaller content assets are combined into larger ones as you move from the bottom up. "A learning object is not just a small piece of content," says director of systems engineering Rich Sutton. "It can be a course, a module, a unit of instruction, or a competency, which is a skill or knowledge for a task."

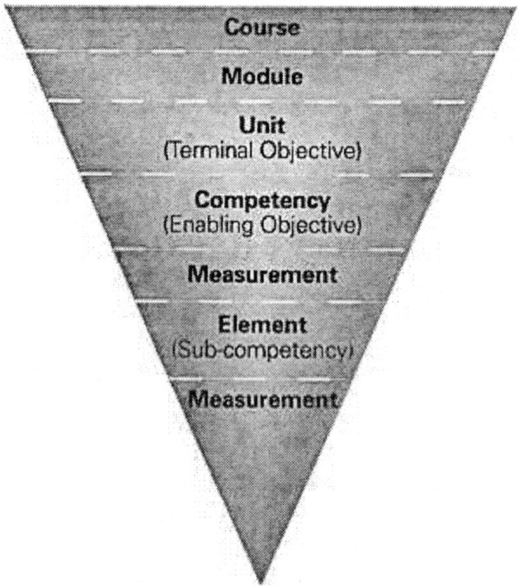

Each TKM hierarchy level can be considered a learning object. That's because TKM can deliver any level individually, down to a single media object, such as a graphic or sound file. From an instructional standpoint, however, TKM considers the dynamic learning object at the competency level.

Within the hierarchy, a competency "should be measurable and have an objective associated with it," says Sutton. "The idea behind the system is to make those competencies digestible pieces of information. A competency could be a [step-by-step] procedure for how to change a tire, or [general] knowledge about how to change a tire," he adds.

In addition, even though the TKM learning object hierarchy is fixed, the system offers some adaptive delivery capabilities. Based on measurement items delivered during the learning experience, the system tracks how quickly each learner absorbs new information and skills. The system then dynamically modifies how and in what sequence it presents the learning object content to each learner.

15
Environmental Education

Environment is the sum total of all the external condition and influences affecting the organism. Environment is the basic life support system. It provides air we breathe, water we drink, food we eat and lord we live. The place, pupil, things and nature that surround any living organism is called its environment. Environment consists of two components – natural and man made. Natural environment consist of biotic and abiotic component. Biotic component consist of all living beings all plants, animals, fish and all microorganism. Abiotic component consist of all non-living elements like soil, air, water, energy and sunlight, man-made environment consist of language, custom, venicle, etc.

Environment education is education, through about and for environment. According to the International Union for the

Conservation of Nature and Natural Resources Commission of Education "Environmental Education is the process recognizing values an clarifying concepts in order to develop skills and attitudes necessary to understand and appreciate the interrelatedness among man, his culture and his biophysical surroundings".

Environmental Education is a permanent process and through this individual and community gain awareness about the environment and acquire skill, knowledge and experience about it. The crucial aim of environmental education is the development of behaviour which is in according with environmental needs.

Environmental education programs often aim to change people's perceptions about the value of the natural world and to teach how to change environmental behaviors, such as getting people to recycle or how to build eco-friendly dwellings.

Environmental education (EE) refers to organized efforts to teach about how natural environments function and, particularly, how human beings can manage their behaviour and ecosystems in order to live sustainably. The term is often used to imply education within the school system, from primary to post-secondary. However, it is sometimes used more broadly to include all efforts to educate the public and other audiences, including print materials, websites, media campaigns, etc. Related disciplines include outdoor education and experiential education.

Environmental education is a learning process that increases people's knowledge and awareness about the environment and associated challenges, develops the necessary skills and expertise to address the challenges, and fosters attitudes, motivations, and commitments to make informed decisions and take responsible action (UNESCO, Tbilisi Declaration, 1978).

In Western-style environmental education, the focus is mostly on understanding ways in which humans and human systems impact on the environment and non-human natural systems. However, it is also important to teach and understand the impact of natural systems on humans and human society.

15.1. Goals of Environmental Education

Environmental education programs often aim to:

(i) help students develop factual knowledge about the natural environment, particularly with regard to how ecosystems work and human impacts on the natural environment;
(ii) foster more positive perceptions about the value of the natural world;
(iii) develop eco-friendly habits, such as getting people to recycle and to produce less waste
(iv) engage students in environmental rejuvenation projects and action
(v) develop students' psychological and spiritual relationship with nature.

15.2. History

The roots of environmental education can be traced back as early as the 18th century when Jean-Jacques Rousseau stressed the importance of an education that focuses on the environment in Emile: or, On Education. Several decades later, Louis Agassiz, a Swiss-born naturalist, echoed Rousseau's philosophy as he encouraged students to "Study nature, not books." These two influential scholars helped lay the foundation for a concrete environmental education program, known as Nature study, which took place in the late 19th century and early 20th century.

The nature study movement used fables and moral lessons to help students develop an appreciation of nature and embrace the natural world. Anna Botsford Comstock, the head of the Department of Nature Study at Cornell University, was a prominent figure in the nature study movement and wrote the Handbook for Nature Study in 1911, which used nature to educate children on cultural values. Cornstock and the other leaders of the movement, such as Liberty Hyde Bailey, helped Nature Study garner tremendous amounts of support from community leaders, teachers, and scientists and change the science curriculum for children across the United States.

A new type of environmental education, Conservation Education, emerged as a result of the Great Depression and Dust Bowl during the 1920s and 1930s. Conservation Education dealt with the natural world in a drastically different way from Nature Study because it focused on rigorous scientific training rather than natural history. Conservation Education was a major scientific management and planning tool that helped solve social, economic, and environmental problems during this time period.

The modern environmental education movement, which gained significant momentum in the late 1960s and early 1970s, stems from Nature Study and Conservation Education. During this time period, many events – such as Civil Rights, the Vietnam War, and the Cold War – placed Americans at odds with one another and the U.S. government. However, as more people began to fear the fallout from radiation, the chemical pesticides mentioned in Rachel Carson's Silent Spring, and the significant amounts of air pollution and waste, the public's concern for their health and the health of their natural environment led to a unifying phenomenon known as environmentalism.

The first article about environmental education as a new movement appeared in Phi Delta Kappan in 1969, authored by James A. Swan. A definition of "Environmental Education" first appeared in Educational Digest in March 1970, authored by William Stapp. Stapp later went on to become the first Director of Environmental Education for UNESCO, and then the Global Rivers International Network.

Ultimately, the first Earth Day on April 22, 1970 – a national teach-in about environmental problems – paved the way for the modern environmental education movement. Later that same year, President Nixon passed the National Environmental Education Act, which was intended to incorporate environmental education into K-12 schools. Then, in 1971, the National Association for Environmental Education (now known as the North American Association for Environmental Education) was created to improve environmental literacy by providing resources to teachers and promoting environmental education programs.

Internationally, environmental education gained recognition when the UN Conference on the Human Environment held in Stockholm, Sweden, in 1972, declared environmental education must be used as a tool to address global environmental problems. The United Nations Education Scientific and Cultural Organization (UNESCO) and United Nations Environment Program (UNEP) created three major declarations that have guided the course of environmental education.

Environmental education (EE) has been considered an additional or elective subject in much of traditional curriculum.

At the elementary school level, environmental education can take the form of science enrichment curriculum, natural history field trips, community service projects, and participation in outdoor science schools. EE policies assist schools and organizations in developing and improving environmental education programs that provide citizens with an in-depth understanding of the environment. School related EE policies focus on three main components: curricula, green facilities, and training.

Schools can integrate environmental education into their curricula with sufficient funding from EE policies. This approach – known as using the "environment as an integrating context" for learning – inserts environmental education into the core subjects and thus environmental education does not take time away from other important subjects, such as art, gym, or music. In addition to funding environmental curricula in the classroom, environmental education policies allot the financial resources for hands-on, outdoor learning. These activities and lessons help address and mitigate "nature deficit disorder", as well as encourage healthier lifestyles.

Green schools, or green facility promotion, are another main component of environmental education policies. Greening school facilities cost, on average, a little less than 2 percent more than creating a traditional school, but payback from these energy efficient buildings occur within only a few years. Environmental education policies help reduce the relatively small burden of the initial start-up costs for green schools. Green school policies also provide grants for modernization, renovation, or repair of older school facilities. Additionally, healthy food options are also a central aspect of green schools. These policies specifically focus on bringing freshly prepared food, made from high-quality, locally grown ingredients into schools.

In secondary school, environmental curriculum can be a focused subject within the sciences or is a part of student interest groups or clubs. At the undergraduate and graduate level, it can be considered its own field within education, environmental studies, environmental science and policy, ecology, or human/cultural ecology programs.

Environmental education is not restricted to in-class lesson plans. There are numerous ways children can learn about the environment in which they live. From experiential lessons in the school yard and field trips to national parks to after-school green clubs and school wide sustainability projects, the environment is a topic which is readily and easily accessible. Furthermore, celebration of Earth Day or participation in EE week (run through the National Environmental Education Foundation) is a great way to dedicate your lessons to environmental education. To be most effective, promote a holistic approach and lead by example, using sustainable practices in the classroom and school grounds and encouraging students and parents to bring environmental education into their home.

The final aspect of environmental education policies, but certainly not least important, is training individuals to thrive in a sustainable society. In addition to building a strong relationship with nature, American citizens must have the skills and knowledge to succeed in a 21st century workforce. Thus, environmental education policies fund both teacher training and worker training initiatives. Teachers must be trained to effectively teach and incorporate environmental studies in their curricula. On the other hand, the current workforce must be trained or re-trained so that they can adapt to the new green economy. Environmental education policies that fund training programs are critical in educating citizens to prosper in a sustainable society.

15.3. Objectives of Environmental Education

The objectives of Environmental Education can be subsumed in three domains by Bloom. They are given below:

The objective of Environmental Education in cognitive domain are:

1. To help individuals require knowledge of the immediate environment.
2. To evaluate the utilization of physical and human resources and suggest remedial measures.
3. To diagnose the different causes of environmental pollution and to suggest remedial measures.

The objectives of Environmental Education in affective domain are:

1. To appreciate the gift of nature

2. To value the cleanliness and purity of our environment.
3. To help argue interest in the flora and fauna of the near and also distant environment.

The objectives of Environmental Education on psychomotor domain are

1. To participate in reforestation programmes.
2. To participate in programmes aimed at preventing soil erosion, minimizing air, water and noise pollution.
3. To participate in changing neighbourhood

In summary, environmental education has the following objectives

- *Awareness* – to help social groups and individuals acquire an awareness and sensitivity to the total environment and its allied problems.
- *Knowledge* – to help social groups and individuals gain a variety of experiences in and acquire a basic understanding of the environment and its associated problems.
- *Attitudes* – to help social groups and individuals acquire a set of values and feelings of concern for the environment and motivation for actively participating in environmental improvement and protection.
- *Skills* – to help social groups and individuals acquire the skills for identifying and solving environmental problems.
- *Participation* – to help provide social groups and individuals with an opportunity to be actively involved at all levels in working toward resolution of environmental problems.

15.4. Need for Environmental Education

Some Educational principles that support the inclusion of Environmental Education in school curriculum are given below:

1. Environmental Education helps in programming learning experience from simple to complex.
2. It helps children to proceed from indefinite ideas to definite ideas.

3. It helps to proceed from concrete to abstract.
4. It helps in the ordering of learning experience from the empirical to rational.
5. It helps to child in the process of self development.
6. It helps the child to follow the same sequence of as existed in the education of mankind.
7. It helps to create pleasurable experience and excitements in students.
8. It helps to make the child's education problem based for understanding the environment and the hazards of its pollution.
9. Environmental Education helps to know the principle of social relevance. Its relevance to man's interaction with physical and social environment and its relevant to change in human attitudes etc.

Since Environmental Education enhances the ability to respond to environmentally challenges, quality of education and also it protect the human health and build better citizens it is more relevant in school curriculum.

15.5. Strategies for Effective Environmental Education

1. Environmental Education should be an integral part of each stage of Formal Education right from pre-primary to the university stage.
2. It is a lifelong process and should not remain confined into formal system of education. It should form a part of non-formal education, adult education, farmers training etc.
3. Environmental education during early years should based on the sense of wonder and joy of discovery. Children should be given an opportunity to bond with nature and feed it.
4. The secondary stage curriculum should lay emphasis on awareness of life experiences, conservation and action skills.
5. At the University stage, content must be based on science and technology, environmental engineering, conservation and management, environmental health and social ecology.

15.6. Co-curricular Activities to promote Environmental Awareness

Under NSS and SUPW programmes, some activities can be done. For example,

(a) Cleaning the environment
(b) growing plants
(c) digging pits for the waste in the village
(d) developing sense of sanitation among the villages by organizing cultural programmes.
(e) Non formal education include G.D., lectures, print and electronic media, film and documentaries for effective environmental education.

15.7. Different Approaches of Environmental Education

I. Infusion Approach

It can be done in two ways through interdisciplinary and through multi disciplinary. In inter disciplinary approach Environmental Education is imparted by drawing concepts and inputs from various discipline. Environmental Education is taught as a separate subject that contain the relevant aspect of sociology, economics, science etc.

In multidisciplinary approach environmental topics are infused into other various disciplinary courses.

Eg: We can include environmental topics in chemistry or biology text book and thus impart environmental education as part of the teaching the subject.

II. Problem Solving

It is a method aimed to help the participant to arrive at a solution or alternative solution of a given problem.

Programmes for Environmental Education can be classified into two

(a) Awareness programmes
(b) Action programmes

(a) Awareness programmes

1. Talk, lectures, seminars, discussion in environment problems.
2. Competition in essay and story writing on environmental issues.
3. Nature clubs and Nature study camps
4. Observation of Environmental days, week and months.
5. Visual programmes on environmental issues

(b) Action programmes

1. Conduct annual flower and vegetable shows
2. Organize campus greening programmes
3. Organize field trips, surveys and biological collection.
4. Participants in Social Forestry Programmes and Community Development Programmes.
5. Learning by observing animals and plants in natural settings.

15.8. Techniques for Evaluation and Monitoring

The objective of Environmental Education are to be relieved by employing a variety of techniques and strategies. Success of this depends upon gathering of feedback, scientific evaluation and systematic monitoring.

The process of measurement and evaluation has 3 main function (1) Prognosis (2) Diagnosis and (3) Prediction are relevant in case of Environmental Education also.

In order to ensure that objective and comprehensive evaluation is made possible, four aspects have to be evaluated in effective programmes of environmental education. They are:

1. Educational attainment in term of related awareness, understandings, attitudes and skills.
2. Precise measurement of pollution with regard to air, water, land, sound and radiation and study of these measures on the basis of norms.
3. Assessing the workability of the efforts used for controlling environmental pollution.
4. Appraisal of the possible adverse efforts of human plans and projects designed for development in various domains or environment.

World Wide Environmental Issues

1. Green house effect
2. Ozone depletion
3. Acid Rain
4. Environmental Pollution
   (a) Air pollution
   (b) Water pollution
   (c) Land pollution
   (d) Sound pollution
   (e) Radiation pollution
5. Deforestation

15.9. Environmental Movements in India

As a result of the Lethargic attitude of the Government towards Environmental problems, peoples movements have come to find solutions of the problem such as exploitation of national resources, deforestation, environmental pollution.

The Silent valley Movement

India, a country with the seventh largest landmass in the world, is a land of ancient traditions. With over a billion people and at least 17major languages, the diversity of India in terms of culture and biological wealth is enormous. In spite of rapidly changing lifestyles, the traditions of living in harmony with nature and of environmentally sound practices underpin the lives of most people. It is against this backdrop that the country's EE strategy has been evolved. The Constitution of India explicitly makes environmental conservation a duty. The Central Government and all states within India now have a Ministry or Department of Environment.

Education departments recognize EE as an essential part of education. The law courts of the country have been sympathetic to environmental causes. India has a very large number of very active NGOs who are involved in a variety of activities from policy analysis to school programs; from participatory natural resources management to activism. India continues to be rich in its biodiversity. Agricultural revolution has ensured that food-grain production has not just kept pace with the population increase, but has rather grown faster. With better nutrition and health care, the life expectancy has gone up by almost 3 times since the independence. The per capita income has grown almost 45 times during this period.

But the environment in India faces several challenges too. With poverty and low literacy levels, over 650,000 primary schools and rapidly increasing population, the development and environmental challenges are enormous. India has made considerable strides in slowing down its population growth. But with all efforts, India's annual population increase is equal to the population of Australia. With about 16 per cent of the world population and a little over 2 per cent of its land, there is already enormous pressure on our resources.

But while the population increase puts pressure on resources, the pressure of 'development' is perhaps even greater.

Chipko Movement

It was stated in 1973 against deforestation in the Chamali district of Uttar Pradesh. The movement under the strong leadership of Sardeslal Bahuguna and Chandi Prasad Bhat spread to other parts of the country. This movement is responsible for the enactment of the Forest Protection Act 1980 and the creation of a separate ministry for environment at the centre.

The Narmada Bachao Andolan (NBA)

This was led by Baba Amte and Medha Patkar for the proper rehabilitation of over 1 lakh people evicted on account of the Narmada Valley project.

15.10 Role of Environmental Education in the Indian Context

There are many challenges for environmental educators in India. Apart from the obvious ones of helping strengthen environmental management and conservation, one of the important ones is to bring about awareness of the need that the country develops in less wasteful ways than is the current paradigm. EE is one of the tools that can help India achieve this goal. There are considerable initiatives in EE in India today. There are also several challenges. Some of these are:

The challenge, in a large and diverse country, to find the right blend between centralized and de-centralized efforts and approaches The challenge of reaching out to large numbers cost-effectively The challenge of making environmental considerations relevant and meaningful to various groups The challenge of putting EE on the agenda of educational decision makers The challenge of putting sustainable development concerns high on the agenda of policy makers, and Finding and developing human and financial resources for EE. the above examples, attempts to reflect the kind of environmental challenges India faces, and the wide and rich variety of EE efforts that have been initiated in the country, and also tries to analyze what has worked and why, or for that matter even.

Appreciation and concern for the environment are values that need to be inculcated during the early years of development. Thus EE for children and youth becomes an integral and important part of the EE strategy of any country. India, a land of diversity ecological, biogeographical, cultural, social requires efforts which are rooted in the local context, which present a picture to which the child relates, can provide solutions of which the child can be a part. The following is a case of one such pioneering effort from Kerala.

Bibliography

Allen, D.W, Ryan, K.A. (1969). *Micro-teaching Reading Mass,* Addison Wesley.

Ausubel. D.P. (1962). *Learning by discovery: Educational Leadership,* 20: 113, Nov. 1962.

Bloom's Taxonomy – Learning Domains retrieved from www.business balls.com on March 5, 2007

Dececoo, J.P. (1964). *Educational Technology.* New York: Henry, Holt and Company.

Dembo, M. H.(1977), *Teaching for learning: Applying Educational Psychology in the Classroom.* California: Good Year Publishing Company.

http://tip.psychology.org/ausubel.html

http://www.pgcps.org/~elc/learning1.html

Innovative Science Teaching (for Physical Science Teaching) – Radha Mohan

J.K. Sood (1989). *New Directions in Science Education.* Chandigarh: Kohli Publishers.

Johnson, D.W. and R.T. Johnson. *Cooperation and Competition: Theory and Research.* Edina, MN: Interaction Book Company, 1989.

Johnson, David W., R. Johnson, and E. Holubec. *Circles of Learning: Cooperation in the Classroom.* Edina, MN: Interaction Book Company, 1990.

New Directions in Teaching Secondary School Science–Paul Bettert Hurd

Passi, B.K. (1976), *Becoming Better Teachers,* Baroda : Centre for Advanced Study in Education, M.S. University of Baroda.

Romiszowski, A (1999) The Development of Physical Skills: Instruction in the Psychomotor Domain, Chapter 19, *Instructional Design Theories and Models: A New Paradigm of Instructional Theory,* Volume II, C. M. Reigeluth, Mahwah, NJ, Lawrence Erlbaum Associates

Science Education at Elementary Level – Sachindra Mohan Sahu

Science Teachings in Schools – R.C. Das

Teaching of Physical Science – U.K. Sharma

Teaching of Science- M.S. Yadav

www.funderstanding.com/content/piaget

www.learningandteaching.info/learning/piaget.htm

www.wikipedia.com

Index